The Carpenter's Four-Part Guide to Making Disciples

Glen D. Pierce

Published by CrossVision Missions INT
P.O. Box 132982
Tyler, TX 75713

ISBN-13: 978-0692675557
ISBN-10: 069275558

Table of Contents

Introduction

I was twenty nine years old and I had been faithfully active in church all of my life. I had served on almost every committee, taught Sunday school, and participated in several mission trips and even chaired a mission team serving alongside a church planter in the area I lived. As far as anyone knew I was a poster boy for the Christian life. No one in my church family, not even I realized I was just doing my Christian duty. The truth is all my activity for God was in my own power and by my own will. Church had become monotonous, empty, routine, and void of any excitement. I was slowly exiting and drawing away and I couldn't even see it happening. It was at that point that I was engulfed by the storm that would forever change my life.

Within a one year period my entire life was flipped on end and I was completely lost as to what to do next. I came face to face with the fact that I had put my faith in the Church and missed a relationship with Jesus altogether. I wish I could say this is when my relationship with Christ started. The truth is this is when God revealed his desire to have a relationship with me. He then started to draw me to the place where he could have a relationship with me. It would be six more years and a five hundred mile move before He would draw me to one of his disciples so that I could learn what I was missing.

The overwhelming majority of church members today, are just like I was, sure of their salvation based on an event that took place in their youth. At the same time, a high percentage of these have little to no personal relationship with Jesus. Most are actively involved in a Bible-believing congregation but wonder if there is more to being a Christian than being a faithful member of a church. Although this is a guide to becoming a disciple maker, it does not automatically assume that the student fully understands the basic truths. We need to learn the basics as well as possible in order to fully understand that these foundational truths are as important to every disciple's life as water is to our physical body.

Learning how to recognize evidence of spiritual birth is critical to our seeing ourselves and other believers as children of God. Our close spiritual relationship with Christ is what will draw to us those who desire to be disciples. If we cannot describe our relationship with Jesus in the same way as we describe our relationship with loved ones and close friends, we probably have never experienced the relationship in the way that God wants us to. For the disciple, it is not enough just to know our salvation is secure. Disciples hunger for a close personal relationship with God and they long to guide others into a close relationship as well.

This study guide is intended to go hand and hand with the book, "Fishermen, Carpenters, Mechanics, and Tax Collectors." I believe the main reason most Christians do not participate in the disciple making process is because they simply do not know how to start and even if God does draw someone into their life they do not have a plan or guide to follow. Yes it's true many great books by powerful preachers have been written to assist believers in the disciple making process. I have benefitted much from studying some of these books.

What I have attempted to do is to guide laymen, like myself, to an understanding of how to lead others into a right relationship with Jesus. A disciple's relationship you could say. It's a mistake for laymen to think they are responsible to educate others in all of scripture. When we see ourselves as a part of a disciple making team, rather than a lone wolf disciple maker, we begin to lead others through the first steps and then willingly introduce them to the person who is better equipped to assist them in become a stronger disciple. This guide will assist those who choose to use it, in leading other to understand the basics of a right relationship with God. In other words, it is a guide to lead others through the first steps of being a disciple and eventually a disciple maker.

PART 1

Are You Truly a
Disciple of Christ Jesus?

*"All authority has been given to me, go and make disciples
of all nations…"*
~Jesus Christ
(Matt. 28:18-19)

For us to have a great relationship (a disciple's relationship) with Christ there are some basic truths that we need to learn and gain the understanding of how we incorporate these into our daily lives.

Part one focusses on our need to;

- Identify the evidence of Spiritual birth and see it here and now every day.
- Understand our relationship with God/Jesus in the way God see it.
- Living our lives as a Child of God.
- Living the life of a Disciple of Christ.
- Loving God and each other.

Step 1:

Understanding Our Spiritual Birth and
Our Position in Christ

"Jesus answered, "Truly, truly, I say to you, unless one is born of the water and the Spirit, he cannot enter the Kingdom of God."
(John 3:5)

Before any Christian can fully experience a close personal relationship with Christ, they must realize and be able to identify their own spiritual birth as well as the evidence (fruit) that is a visible part of who we are and what we do as Children of God. It is not enough to be able to say, "I have prayed the sinner's prayer, so I am born again!" Spiritual birth brings about real visible change.

In order to fully experience this magnificent relationship, we must first understand how it works. God is in control of this relationship and if we try to force our will into it we will find ourselves super frustrated and wondering if God is listening at all.

During the course of this first study, we will discover how to identify our spiritual birth, see it in very real and present ways, and enjoy its fruits every day of our lives. We will learn how a relationship with God works, what our position in the relationship is, and what pleases God most in the relationship.

"Truly, truly, I say to you, unless one is born again he cannot see the kingdom of God." ~Jesus
(John 3:3)

In John Chapter 3, Jesus describes this spiritual birth as being like the wind. We cannot tell exactly where the wind comes from or where it is going, but the evidence of the wind is obvious to all.

Read John 3:1-8.

1. What is significant about what Nicodemus says to Jesus? What does it indicate about who he believed Jesus was?

2. Why does Jesus respond with a proclamation saying, "Unless one is born again he cannot see the kingdom of God?" Is he talking about here and now, or is this about heaven after we die physically?

3. What is Jesus teaching in verse 8? Explain how wind compares to spiritual birth?

4. What are some evidences that spiritual birth has taken place in someone's life?

5. How would you describe your spiritual birth to someone who does not know you or your life as a believer?

6. If you had to present a case proving your spiritual birth to a judge, what evidence would you present?

Commentary:

I met Jim about three years ago. He worked in a business I frequent and we struck up a friendship. Jim had grown up in church and, as a boy during a revival, he accepted Christ along with a group of his buddies. Now, as a 50-year-old grandfather, he sits in church every Sunday confused by the words of the preacher and claiming he does not understand scripture. Although Jim is a good man, he has begun to use alcohol on a daily basis and sees himself as frustrated and not sure if salvation is even something we can know for certain.

Like Nicodemus, Jim believes Jesus is of God and he often cries out to understand why he feels empty. Unlike Nic, he has never been confronted with the reality of spiritual birth. For some reason, no one ever helped him determine if, in fact, he had ever truly experienced spiritual birth. He had spent his entire adult life clinging to his public profession as a boy but, other than church attendance, could not give any evidence that he had the Spirit of God in him. He saw the Kingdom of God as something that had not yet come and felt it was completely about a place we will experience after death.

- Nicodemus knew Jesus was of God, but he did not see Him as God.

- Jesus knew Nic did not have what he needed to see the Kingdom of God all around him.

- Jesus describes spiritual birth in a very tangible way that every living person can understand. No matter what condition of life in which we find ourselves, the effects of the wind are obvious even though we cannot fully explain it.

- When we have truly been born of the Spirit of God, the effects are unmistakable.

- We should learn to see the Spirit at work in our lives and embrace it as evidence that we have been born of the Spirit.

- If we learn to identify the Spirit in us, we will be able to describe what our spiritual birth looks like to friends, family, and strangers.

7. **Read Galatians 5** and see if you can build a case for your spiritual birth that will stand in any court, here or in heaven.

Personal Evaluation:

   a. John 3:1-8 helps me to more clearly understand my own salvation because:

Step 2:

Determining Our Relationship to God

"Whoever humbles himself like this child is the greatest in the kingdom of heaven"
(Matthew 18:4)

When you were born to your parents, you were immediately a part of their family. The same is true about spiritual birth and immediately becoming a member of God's family. We enter both as newborn infants completely dependent on our parents to meet every need. However, there is one huge difference in being born into a human family and being born spiritually into God's family. As we mature as humans, our dependence on our parents decreases. But as we mature in our spiritual life, we grow more dependent on God. As we grow and mature in our human bodies, we become equal to our parents. However, as we grow and mature spiritually, we come to realize how far short of God's perfection and glory we fall and we find ourselves more dependent on the Holy Spirit each day.

The truth of this spiritual difference is not taught to us as children in Sunday school or the church, so we may grow up with the concept that just as we have matured and become equal to our parents physically, we have matured and have become adult in our spiritual lives as well. Many Christians have developed a false sense of bold adultness in their relationship to God. This is especially true in the way we approach prayer. We must examine what Jesus teaches to realize it is something very different than an adult-to-adult relationship.

Read Matthew 18:1-3.

1. In verse 1, Jesus responds to the disciple's question. What is He teaching about the relationship with God?

2. These were grown men. What does Jesus mean when He says, "unless you become like children; you will never enter the kingdom of heaven?"

3. Does this passage indicate that our relationship with God only functions correctly with us as a child in relation to our father? Explain.

4. Matthew 18:4 sums up the responsibility we have in the relationship. Explain how spiritual birth leads to humility and makes it possible for us to have a right relationship with God.

"But to all who did receive him, who believed in his name, he gave the right to become children of God."
(John 1:12)

As we share our faith and seek to live as followers of Christ, we will, without a doubt, encounter people who believe all humans are God's children. Even within Christian denominations you will discover people who claim that all who believe that Jesus is who the Bible says He is are God's children. After all, if you are in church every time the doors are open, you must be a child of God, right?

5. According to John 1:12, what do good deeds, right living, wealth, or even faithful church membership have to do with the right to become children of God?

6. Using John 1:12-13, explain what Jesus is saying about what the new birth is *not* of.

Personal Evaluation:

    a.   I began to recognize evidence of my own spiritual birth when:

    b.   I know that others recognize me as a child of God because:

    c.   My personal relationship with God is based on:

Commentary:

Jesus' life and actions are our example of how everything in God's kingdom functions. We must take a long look at how Jesus addressed God the Father. In every relational situation, Jesus is talking to, observing, or directly interacting with His Father. He teaches us to pray to our Father, recognize the authority of our Father, and be completely obedient to God the Father.

In our adultness, we sometimes forget how children and parents interact and we tend to come at God with our "we-are-not-babies-anymore" attitude. That is when God turns a deaf ear to our prayers. That is when He draws our attention to the little child and that child's completely dependent faith. We are humbled when we realize that this is the only way to have a right relationship with God.

Often we become puffed up in our knowledge of scripture and see ourselves as wise and learned. We teach others so we must be treated like a person with a closer relationship with the Lord. We become leaders in the church and make decisions of importance regarding our whole congregation. Surely we must be taking all this to God and having Him approve of our decisions. NOT!

Children simply want to be near their Dad and feel His strong presence. Sure they talk, but He is the only one with the answers and He alone is adult, smart, wise, and learned. Yes, He alone is Holy!

Step 3:

Living as Children of God

But Jesus called them to him, saying, "Let the children come to me, and do not hinder them, for to such belongs the kingdom of God."
(Luke 18:16)

By now you should have a clear picture of both what spiritual birth is and what it means to our relationship with God, as well as who is and who is not a child of God. Now let's discover how we can live like children of God.

Read Romans 8:1-14.

1. What does being set free from the law of sin and death mean to you personally?

2. Describe a person's life that walks not according to the flesh but according to the Spirit.

3. Explain how verse 8 helps us determine how to have a right relationship with God.

4. What should lead or guide the life of a child of God?

5. How do we talk, act, and live like children of God?

"No one born of God makes a practice of sinning, for God's seed abides in him, and he cannot keep on sinning because he has been born of God. By this it is evident who are the children of God, and who are the children of the devil: whoever does not practice righteousness is not of God, nor is the one who does not love his brother."
(1 John 3:9-10)

6. How do our choices, words, and actions reflect on our Father (God) and the family of Christ?

7. Does this verse teach that as a born-again child of God we will never be tempted and or never sin again? Explain.

8. What are the consequences when a child does something wrong and disobeys his or her father?

9. What can a child do that will result in no longer being his father's child?

"If you then, who are evil, know how to give good gifts to your children, how much more will your Father who is in heaven give good things to those who ask him!" (Matthew 7:11)

10. Jesus teaches that God is much more gracious than man. So when God births us into His family and calls us His children, what can we do to no longer be His child?

"If we confess our sins, he is faithful and just to forgive our sin, and to cleanse us from all unrighteousness."
(1 John 1:9)

11. What does this verse instruct us to do to restore our relationship to God the Father if we sin?

12. To who are we instructed to confess and what does that confession look like?

13. Can a person who has received the Spirit of God simply renounce his or her faith, return to a life of sin, and no longer be a child of God? Explain.

Personal Evaluation:

    a.   How does my life tell others that I am a child of God?

    b.   I remain in a right relationship with God by:

Commentary:

Though many celebrities and even religious leaders claim we are all God's children because He made us all, God's Word says something very different. In fact, in John 1:12–13, we learn that even belief in God only gives a person the right to become a child of God. In other words, that is the condition for adoption. Jesus teaches us something here that flies in the face of nature. He points out the difference in how we are physically born and how we are born of God. Being born of flesh is a choice of man and being born of the Spirit is a choice of God. The only part we play in that is receiving the truth of Christ as a part of who we are. God does the rest. Instead of us just claiming to be children of God or being one of our own accord or desire, a birth into God's family must take place.

We are identified as a part of God's family by our actions, choices, and lifestyles. The life of a child of God is not characterized as sinful. Children of God focus on the things of God rather than on personal sin. When we are focused on the things of God, our life reflects those characteristics and the fruits of the Spirit identify what family we are a part of. When we focus on sin, even on not sinning, it is only a matter of time before sin invades our heart.

Step 4:

Living as a Disciple

"By this all people will know that you are my disciples, if you have love for one another."
another."
(John 13:35)

"So Jesus said to the Jews who had believed in him, "If you abide in my word, you are truly my disciples, and you will know the truth, and the truth will set you free." They answered him, "We are offspring of Abraham and have never been enslaved to anyone. How is it that you say, 'You will be set free?' Jesus answered them, "Truly, truly I say to you, everyone who commits sin is a slave to sin. The slave does not remain in the house forever; the son remains forever. So if the Son sets you free, you will be free indeed."
(John 8:31-36)

1. What is the promise Jesus is offering us and what are the conditions to receiving this promise?

2. In what ways have you been enslaved to sin in your past?

3. Some teach that this gives us a freedom is to sin without consequences, rather than freedom from sin. How does this teaching relate to Jesus saying, "...everyone who commits sin is a slave to sin? The slave does not remain in the house forever?"

4. What are the benefits of seeing ourselves as children of God, filling our minds with the Word of God, and living in a way that honors our Father God?

5. What will be the results if we continue to see ourselves as sinners (even saved sinners) and let thoughts of sin continue to remain in our minds?

Read Matthew 4:19, Matthew 10:38, Mark 8:34, John 12:26.

6. What are some of the conditions Jesus gives for being His disciple?

7. In Mark 8:34, Jesus says, "If anyone would come after me, let him deny himself..." What does this mean to you on a personal level?

Truly, truly, I say to you, unless a grain of wheat falls into the earth and dies, it remains alone; but if it dies, it bears much fruit. Whoever loves his life loses it, and whoever hates his life in this world will keep it for eternal life. If anyone serves me, he must follow me; and where I am, there will my servant be also. If anyone serves me, the Father will honor him."
(John 12:24-26)

8. Jesus' physical body was crucified and resurrected. Now He lives and has placed His Spirit in many lives. What is Jesus teaching His disciples about this life here and now?

9. How does Jesus characterize His disciple three times in verse 26?

Read Luke 6:40.

10. What is the goal of a disciple?

11. How have the previous verses helped you to understand what it means to follow Jesus?

The Apostle Paul had all that this life had to offer. Then he met Jesus and became His disciple. Listen closely to Paul's testimony to the world in Galatians 2:20:

> *"I have been crucified with Christ. It is no longer I*
> *who live, but Christ who lives in me. The life I now live in*
> *the flesh I live by faith in the Son of God, who loved me and*
> *gave himself for me."*

2. Paul was not physically crucified. So what does he mean and how does that reflect on the verses we studied in John 12?

Read Matthew 10:37.

13. Who is Jesus teaching, and what is He teaching them about relationships?

14. Can you see yourself as one of these disciples?

Read Luke 14:25-33.

15. Who is Jesus talking to?

16. What have His disciples given up to follow Him?

17. How does the way Jesus addresses the crowd tell us what his disciples have already done? Explain. (Is Jesus saying those in the crowd cannot be disciples?)

18. Is Jesus testing some in the crowd or is He simply revealing His strategic plan in identifying who He will trust with the Gospel? Explain.

19. Can you see yourself more easily as being one in the crowd or one of His disciples that has given everything up to follow Him?

Personal Evaluation:

a. I am willing to be a disciple of Jesus Christ! I know to be His disciple; I must do what most Christians simply will not do. I must discipline myself to do the following:

b. In order to go all the way as a disciple of Jesus it could cost me:

Commentary:
Very simply, it should cost us everything to be a disciple of Jesus. Why? The answer is that we, in our sinful nature, have nothing that is holy to contribute to God. In other words, we have nothing God wants or can use. He alone is holy and He alone chooses who will be His disciples. He will not choose anyone who clings to anything in this sinful world.

His disciples had given everything up to be identified with Him and, as history records, all of them were martyred for following Him as Lord of their lives. We may not be martyred, but we must be crucified with Christ to this world.

Step 5:

Loving Jesus and Each Other

"You shall love the Lord your God with all your heart and with all your soul and with all your strength and with all your mind, and your neighbor as yourself."
(Luke 10:27)

Read John 14:15-24.

1. What is the first step to loving Jesus?

2. What is promised to those who love Him and keep His commands?

3. What commands do you believe Jesus is referring to?

4. Research the Gospels and list as many of the commands that Jesus gives us that you can.

"As the Father has loved me, so have I loved you. Abide in my love. If you keep my commandments, you will abide in my love, just as I have kept my Father's commandments and abide in his love. Now remain in my love. If you keep my commands, you will remain in my love, just as I have kept my Father's commands and remain in his love. These things I have spoken to you, that my joy may be in you, and that your joy may be full. This is my commandment, that you love one another as I have loved you. Greater love has no one than this, that someone lay down his life for his friends. You are my friends if you do what I command you. No longer do I call you servants, for the servant does not know what his master is doing; but I have called you friends, for all that I have heard from my Father I have made known to you. "
(John 15: 9-15)

"These things I command you, so that you will love one another." (John 15:17)

5. Describe how Jesus demonstrated His love for the Father.

6. How will you remain in the love of God?

7. How do we demonstrate our love for our friends?

Commentary:

True love cannot be faked. True love comes from God and is always characterized by sacrifice. If we love God, we have no problem losing all we own for His name's sake. If we love God, we will obey His commands, we will live according to His Word, and His Spirit will dwell in us. I suggest we pay close attention to 1 John 4:7-8 and make this truth the staple of our lives. If you want to identify a disciple of Christ, look for the one who truly loves other believers and puts their interests above his or her own.

The Spirit of God in us causes us to love and a disciple can no more hide from that than a zebra can hide his stripes. Love runs through the disciple's veins and energizes his life for the glory of His Father and Lord.

Personal Evaluation.

Part one of this Guide has taught me:

PART 2

The Constitution of
Righteousness

"Everyone then who hears these words of mine and does them will be like a
wise man who built his house on the rock." ~Jesus
(Matthew 7:24)

The Commission of Christ to Every Disciple

"And Jesus came and said to them, "All authority in heaven and on earth has been given to me. Go therefore and make disciples of all nations, baptizing them in the name of the Father and of the Son and of the Holy Spirit, teaching them to observe all that I have commanded you. And behold, I am with you always, to the end of the age."
(Matthew 28:18-20)

Part 2 is all about learning to surrender our will in obedience to Christ.

For a person to consider themselves a disciple they must first answer the question "Who has authority over my life?"

1. According to Romans 10:9, who is Lord of your life?

2. Describe what it means for you personally to have Jesus as Lord of your life.

Jesus' life is a living example to every disciple as to what it means to live under the lordship or the authority of God Almighty.

"If you keep my commandments, you will abide in my love, just as I have kept my Father's commandments and abide in his love."
(John 15:10)
"Whoever does not love me does not keep my words. And the word that you hear is not mine but the Father's who sent me."
(John 14:24)

Jesus lived so much under the authority of the Father that even His words were not His own. He spoke only what the Father gave Him to say. Read the following verses and after each verse write out the teaching or command and list the promises Jesus gives to every disciple.

John 14:21.

John 14:12.

John 15:5-7.

Matthew 28:18-20.

The Foundation

Every good builder starts by building a strong sound foundation. He does this by paying attention to the details. The foundational truths for every disciple to live by were first given to the 12 disciples just after Jesus had fed the five thousand and is more commonly known as the Sermon on the Mount.

Read Matthew 4:23-5:1.

Jesus had become a rock star with huge crowds of groupies following Him whenever He was around. The crowd gathered in hopes of seeing another miracle.

1. Describe what Jesus does when He sees the crowd.

2. What do His disciples do?

3. Can you see yourself as one of the disciples or would it be easier to place yourself in the crowd? Explain.

The Sermon on the Mount

Lesson 1
The Beatitudes

Read Matthew 5:3-12.

1. The adverb "blessed" ties all these verses together. What is your understanding of the word "blessed?"

2. Who is blessed? The person who demonstrates these characteristics, God, or both? Explain.

3. Define each characteristic found in the following 10 verses:

    a. Matt. 5:3—poor in spirit

    b. Matt. 5:4— those who mourn

    c. Matt. 5:5— the meek

d. Matt. 5:6—hunger and thirst for righteousness

e. Matt. 5:7— the merciful

f. Matt. 5:8— the pure in heart

g. Matt. 5:9— the peacemakers

h. Matt. 5:10—those persecuted for righteousness

i. Matt. 5:11, 12— persecuted for Christ

4. What is important about the order in which Jesus teaches these characteristics?

5. What characteristics do you struggle with most at this point in your life?

6. As a disciple, what steps must you take to ensure that your life reflects all of these characteristics?

Personal Exercise: Read the book of John and, on a separate sheet of paper, write out a list of points (scriptures, statements, commands, etc.) about which you have spiritual questions. Then do a self-evaluation to determine to what degree you are spiritually dependent on God.

Commentary:

This sermon is the equivalent of the constitution that will govern the Kingdom of God both now and for eternity, announced by Jesus Christ and recorded here for His disciples, both present and those who would become disciples in the future. This proclamation is not and will never be intended for the crowd! Jesus must be more than a rock star. He must be Lord of your life. These are the rules of conduct and directives for righteous living that will forever dictate the decisions and choices of true followers and Disciples of Christ.

Blessed is a word that means much more than "happiness." Happiness is temporal, momentary, and often followed by the opposite emotion, sadness. Blessed is an eternal inner peace and joy that is a gift from God revealing He is pleased. True blessedness permeates the lives within the Kingdom of God.

Matthew 5:3 – Poor in spirit: Complete and utter spiritual dependence on God. All other characteristics, abilities to choose rightly, and expressions of Christlikeness fall on this truth. We must learn to come back to this first principle in each and every time of spiritual need and each and every time we make decisions that reflect on Christ as our Lord.

Personal Questions:
a. Did Christ teach this first because He knew we cannot make righteous choices unless we are willing to depend on Him?
b. What are some steps I can take to maintain spiritual dependence on God?
c. What does God promise the spiritually poor?

Matthew 5:4 – Mourn: This can only be understood through time spent with Christ as He interacts with the lost and hell-bound majority of humanity. When Jesus looks upon His creation and knows they are headed to an eternity in hell, He is heartbroken and mourns for them.

Example: Wendy had been on mission several times and sharing the gospel was her passion. One day while ministering to and sharing her faith with one broken life after another, she was suddenly overcome with a huge burden of compassion for the lost and hurting people she had been encountering. Many of them had rejected Christ. As her tears began to flow uncontrollably, she realized this is how Jesus feels when He encounters hard-hearted and lost people.

Personal Questions:
a. Does God, who offers eternal life, mourn when an unbeliever dies?
b. Does Jesus know where those who reject Him will spend eternity?
c. How do we come to understand how God feels when His salvation is rejected?

Matthew 5:5 – Meek: A gentleness that comes only from the Spirit of Christ living in someone. Many of these people would normally be characterized as strong-willed, gruff, or even volatile, but when the Spirit of Christ comes into their lives, they become as gentle as Christ Himself. On this earth, the meek may only see oppression and abuse, but they will inherit the new earth as their home.

Example: John is a highly decorated and recently retired Marine Captain. Most of the soldiers who have served under him say he is a mild-mannered hero willing to die for any one of his troops. However, John would say, "Only by the grace of God am I fully prepared to die and I will not purposely harm others."

Personal Questions:
a. What is the difference between meekness and weakness?
b. Identify a time when Jesus demonstrated meekness?
c. How does my life reflect the meekness of Christ?

Matthew 5:6 – Hunger and thirst for righteousness: Those who have a deep desire for holiness in their personal lives and in their Christian relationships with others, including their church. They are easily identified as honest, of high integrity, and just among all people.

Personal Questions:
a. How does a hunger for righteousness differ from being religious?
b. How does my desire to be righteous affect my relationship with Jesus?

Matthew 5:7 – Merciful: The key action of all Christians is to reach out in compassion and help those in need or struggling; especially those who are helpless or cannot help themselves. Keep in mind, Jesus never let a funeral procession pass by without performing the most merciful act that could be performed—restoration of life. In the judgment of believers, when all works are reviewed, those who have not shown mercy will not receive mercy.

Personal Questions:
a. Do opportunities to show mercy cross my path every day?
b. What can I do to better recognize the needs of others?
c. What have I experienced that will help me to show mercy to others going through a similar experience?

Matthew 5:8 – Pure in heart: This is not about being guiltless and is much deeper than a childlike innocence. It is a clean and pure conscience. This speaks of those whose motives are in line with the purity of Christ and whose thoughts are holy. In Scripture, these people have supernatural visions or are spoken to by God.

Personal Questions:
a. How willing am I to go out of my way and take a risk for others?
b. Will God alone be glorified if I do this?

c. How do I help others anonymously?

Matthew 5:9 – Peacemakers: Those who actively intervene to make peace. The natural approach is to watch from the sidelines, while the divine approach is to take positive action to promote or bring about peace, even if it means personal trial and abuse. They are not necessarily identified as children of God because they are peacemakers. That only comes through Spiritual birth. However, the true sons of God are characterized as being peacemakers.

Personal Questions:
a. Does intervening in conflicts within the body of Christ come natural to me or is that something I have to force myself to do?
b. Can I identify a time when God drew me into the role of peacemaker?

Matthew 5:10 – Persecuted for righteousness sake: Treated wrongly because of their righteous living as well as their stance against unrighteousness. (Example: Do some of your friends dislike you because you are against homosexuality, abortion, or even voting for a certain political candidate who stands for the same unrighteous values?)

Personal Questions:
a. What exactly am I willing to stand up and take persecution for?
b. How do I reach out and love those who disagree and are angry with me?
c. How will I react if no one else in my family or church stands for righteousness with me?

Matthew 5:11 – Persecuted on account of Christ—Claiming Christ in a hostile world is asking for this type of persecution. Being persecuted because of your Christian faith or attachment to Christ is not about the level of the threat to your person. It is all about how steadfast you will be when faced with denouncing Jesus as Lord of your life. This is not only talking about those faced with torture or death but would also include anyone who has experienced an attack for being a Christian.

Personal Questions:
a. How far am I willing to go for Christ?
b. How does my life reflect this Christ-like attitude?
c. Can I even be counted among those persecuted for Jesus?

Food for thought:

- Spiritual poverty equals Kingdom riches.

- Mourners shall be comforted—all believers' sorrow is limited to here and now on earth. Revelation 21:4 tells us that God will wipe away our tears.

- A temperate man who controls his strength through meekness will one day rule in the new earth.

- The righteous will come to know eternal satisfaction.

- The mercy we show will return to us from the hand of God Himself both now and in eternity.

- Our motives are to please God alone and one day we will see Jesus face-to-face.

- Peace is our passion and we will feel the arms of the Father hold us as His own children.

- Enduring those who know not what they do, we will one day be at home in Heaven.

- Nothing can keep us from claiming Christ as our Lord and our crowns will be laid at His feet alone. Whatever reward He has will be much more than we are worthy of.

Personal Evaluation:

   a.   In view of the blessed attitudes of Christ sermon I feel my strongest points are:

   b.   In view of the blessed attitudes of Christ sermon I feel my weakest points are:

Personal Exercise:

Focus your attention for one full day on each of the B-attitudes. **Example:** Day 1-Blessed are the poor in Spirit. Keep a record of how many times a day you subconsciously pray asking God to help you.

Lesson 2
Salt and Light

Read Matthew 5:13-16.

"You are the salt of the earth, but if salt has lost its taste, how shall its saltiness be restored?"
(Matthew 5:13)

1. List five uses for salt:

2. Describe what life in the days Jesus walked on earth would be like without salt.

3. Jesus announces that His disciples are as important to humanity's salvation as salt is to the preservation of elements. In its spiritual context, how would you define what Jesus means by the phrase, "If salt loses its taste?"

4. Let's say Jesus' disciples understood what He meant when He said they were the salt of the earth. Do you believe they understood how they could lose their saltiness and become irrelevant and have no effect on men? Explain.

5. How can anyone who loses their witness become effective again?

6. What if we read this verse according to its relevancy to the Gospel by changing the word "salt" to "good news" and "saltiness" to "goodness"? Write it out.

"You are the light of the world."
(Matthew 5:14)

7. If the whole earth was pitch dark and you held the only source of light, how popular would you be?

8. In Matthew 5:14 and 15, Jesus uses a metaphoric description of the wrong and right ways to use light. What does this metaphor teach us about what disciples should do or not do with our lives in Christ?

9. How does this teaching relate to your personal ministry as a disciple of Christ?

10. How does being the salt of the earth and the light of the world relate to the Godly characteristics described in Matthew 5:3-12?

Personal Exercise:

Approach at least one person that might not know you are a disciple of Jesus and simply say to them, "Do you know how much Jesus loves you?" Afterwards, journal the experience below.

Commentary:

Salt is a mineral that enhances flavor, seasons, and brings out the best in foods. Salt preserves freshness and stops corruption and poisoning. At that time, salt was more valuable than gold and even a small amount of it gave the one who possessed it great bargaining power.

The disciples easily understood the concept that Jesus was pointing out. He was proclaiming their value as He panned his hand across the horizon toward the crowd. Among the crowd of onlookers who, for the most part, wanted to see Jesus do a miracle, the disciples were God's salt to preserve truth and righteousness. These men would be entrusted with the power of God (Romans 1:16), i.e. the Gospel. As they lived out the spiritual characteristics which He had just taught them in the beatitudes, their greatest function and His purpose for their lives would be revealed.

Today, salt is refined down into a chemical compound in such a way that all of the natural body that would have been used to make a base for footpaths once it lost its saltiness in the day of Jesus no longer exists. If salt losses its saltiness today, nothing remains. Similarly, if a Christian ruins his witness through indulgence in sin, the truth of his words are of no value at all.

Jesus then shifts His attention to something more relevant to each and every one of these men, whether or not they understood the salt metaphor: Light in a dark world. Jesus taught and continues to teach that He is the light of the world and if they remain in Him, and He in them, they themselves are the light of the world wherever they find themselves.

The disciples' lives will be as contrasting to the corrupt world as light is to darkness. But they must not live concealed in some dark corner, seen only by those who search for it, nor hide their lives under the cover of a building (bowl) that serves to limit their effectiveness. They must be as visible as city lights stretched out across a hilltop and seen for many miles, set up on a high point in a room or aimed at providing light to all who come into it.

Their light, their testimony, reflects Christ, the Light of the world, and when their lives are lifted up, He is lifted to light the darkness and draws men to Himself. Their lives will be a ministry of Christian character which speaks far beyond the reach of words. The beatitudes of their spiritual lives will speak much louder than persuasive words alone.

Personal Evaluation:

a. If I were asked to provide evidence that my life serves to preserve righteousness among the people of the community I live in, what evidence would I give?

b. What changes (lifestyle, language, associations) can I make today that will cause my life to be a greater reflection of the Light of the world (Jesus)?

Personal Exercise: Ask a complete stranger (waitress, fireman, police officer, teacher, or obviously lonely person) if you might pray for them and ask something specific for them. Be sure that you address your prayer in the name of the one and only Savior, Jesus. Record the experience. (Use a separate sheet of paper, if necessary.)

Lesson 3
The Fulfillment of the Law

Read Matthew 5:17-20.

1. What do you believe the disciples understood Jesus to mean by "the Law or the Prophets?"

2. How is "the Law or the Prophets" different to you and me today?

3. If you were one of the disciples and you heard Jesus say, "Until heaven and earth pass away," what would you think He was referring to?

4. How should we today view this statement: "Until heaven and earth pass away?" Is it an unfulfilled prophecy or something significant to the disciples at the time?

5. What is significant about Jesus starting verse 18 with the statement, "For truly, I say to you?"

6. What is so important about the way Jesus defines the Law as eternal by saying, "not an iota, not a dot, will pass from the Law until all is accomplished?"

7. How can a person break a law that they know nothing about?

8. How do we avoid breaking commandments or teacher others to avoid the same?

9. Is Jesus teaching or not teaching that we should desire to be great in the Kingdom of God? Explain.

10. What does consistent obedience to God's commands develop in our lives?

11. Verse 20 is a concluding truth that comes about as a result of understanding Jesus' role in righteousness. Once again He states, "For I tell you." What is the truth taught in this passage of Scripture and how does that truth affect our righteousness?

Commentary:

The disciples were not ignorant men. They were, like most Jews, very knowledgeable of the Mosaic Law. In fact, most of the Jews were known as strict followers of the Ten Commandments handed down by Moses. Just because they were fishermen, farmers, carpenters, and a tax collector does not indicate that they were unintelligent zombies following the crowd. Their primary prophet would have been Moses and Exodus 21-30, Leviticus, and Deuteronomy would have been common topics at every one of their dinner tables.

The major difference in what these men believed about the Law and what Jesus is teaching here is that the Law was a means of salvation until the Messiah came, conquered, and ruled with a new set of laws. Accordingly, the belief that Moses and the Ten Commandments would not be relevant to the new set of laws is not at all what Jesus is teaching here.

Jesus was announcing that the Law was the one thing that no human could fulfill or keep. Therefore, it proved that not only could the Jew not save himself, neither could any other race of man. When Jesus says, "I have come to fulfill the law," whether they understood or not, He is literally saying, I am the completion of the Law.

To you and me, this should become our source of faith. Because Jesus has done what no man could do, He alone becomes our means of salvation. Go back to the first beatitude and understand that our salvation is completely dependent on what Christ has done.

The disappearance of heaven and earth is a prophecy not just here within Jesus' teaching on the mount. Throughout Jesus' ministry He prophesizes the passing away of the earth and the heavens as we know them. When Jesus says the meek will inherit the earth, He in no way means that those with His characteristic of meekness will inherit a corrupt sinful earth. The meek are the strong with supernatural self-control that permits the Spirit of God to control their emotions. These are the ones who will lead and rule the new earth.

This teaching would be challenged by the Jewish leaders of the day and distorted by the religious fame seekers through the ages. However, it all boils down to the fact that the Law will reveal those who are true followers of Christ. Throughout New Testament teaching, obedience to all God's Law is taught and Jesus clearly teaches that God's Laws are not dictated by the traditional benefits of men.

Jesus knew man's heart and He knew their tendencies would be to become relaxed with God's commands and even find ways to explain them away. So He greatly emphasizes the fact that breaking even one law and teaching anyone to do the same is an expensive eternal mistake, not in regard to a person's salvation but in regard to their eternal inheritance.

The goal is not for us to be as righteous as religious men but rather to have the righteousness of Christ. Obedience to the commands of God's Word will result in a high eternal position. This is not necessarily a high governmental position but a greater relationship with God. It is our relationship with Christ based on our dependency, obedience, and faith in Christ that will give us entrance into His presence in the Kingdom of Heaven.

Personal Evaluation:

    a. How does this passage agree with or conflict with what I have learned about Old Testament Law?

    b. What can I do today that will make God's commands more relevant to my life and relationships with others?

Lesson 4
Murder, Adultery, Divorce and Oaths

Read Matthew 5:21-37.

1. What is the significance of Jesus starting His teaching with "You have heard that it was said to those of old?

2. What is the root source of the act of murder?

3. What law is Jesus amending and where do we find this law in OT Scripture?

4. What advice does Jesus give in dealing with anger?

5. Does the Mosaic Law prohibit adultery?

6. How can a person be proud of the fact that they have never committed adultery and yet be guilty of adultery?

7. What does Jesus identify as the root of adultery?

8. When Jesus says in verse 39, "if your right eye causes you to sin, tear it out and throw it away," is He advocating self-mutilation? Why does He say this?

9. How important is it for us to be self-disciplined and devoted to right thinking? Why?

10. What is the larger significance of Jesus teaching sin through thought?

11. How does what Jesus teaches about divorce differ from the Jewish practice of the day and the practice of today?

12. What judgment is a man under who divorces his wife for anything other than adultery?

13. What is Jesus teaching about judgment of sin upon the man who divorces for something other than adultery?

14. Describe an oath to the Lord.

15. What does it mean to swear by something?

16. What is the only answer God will accept to His commands?

17. How does this teaching relate to the beatitude of blessed are the pure in heart?

Commentary:
The phrase "you have heard it was said" is Jesus' way of teaching without arrogance. Like the Pharisees, Jesus easily could have proclaimed, "The Ten Commandments I passed down through the prophet Moses say...." Jesus is not a Pharisee and He does not teach out of prideful need for recognition. However, He softly reminds them of what they have been taught about the Mosaic Law. At the same time, He is pointing out that the Pharisees proudly announce they have never

broken the Ten Commandments by committing murder but have broken them through the angry treatment of their subjects.

Murder. In the Kingdom of Heaven, the law starts at the source of the act. Murder is born out of anger. Therefore, Jesus makes an amendment to the Mosaic Law "thou shalt not murder" when He says, "but I say to you that everyone who is angry with his brother will be liable to judgment." In fact, He literally points out three forms of anger. First, is anger in one's thoughts or in one's heart without an outward act, possibly even without just cause. Second, is verbal attack witnessed by others that may cause you to be taken to court. Third, is an outward damning of a person, literally wishing they were dead and in hell.

Jesus is clearly teaching that anger contains the seeds of murder, abusive language contains the spirit of murder, and cursing or damning language implies the very desire to murder. These are progressions of anger that will result in stiff judgments under the Law.

Jesus goes on to proclaim that if we want God to accept our gifts and offerings, we must first be right with all other believers. Also, do it quickly. Do not let it escalate to the point of being brought to court. When you are not right with men, God does not want to hear the excuse and He will not accept an unrepentant heart. This even speaks to our unwillingness to admit we are wrong. If we don't see it as harmful, it may escalate into something much greater that will certainly cost us greatly.

Adultery. This act is one of the big ten. Jesus amends the commandment to include the root of the sin which is a lustful heart. Many men, who in outward appearance are good, respectable, and well thought of as faithful husbands, lust after women other than their wives in their hearts and minds. Jesus is addressing the thoughts of sexual lust as the source of adultery. People do not sit around thinking of adultery or ways to hurt their spouse through adultery. Rather, they permit sexual thoughts to stay on their minds and they dwell on them until they are eventually lived out in the form of adulterous affairs.

We must be willing to go to great extremes to stop the lustful thought process. Jesus very clearly is not telling us to cut out our eyes for looking at women lustfully. He is, however, saying that by thinking we can maintain a pure heart by simply avoiding the act of adultery without dealing severely with the thoughts that lead to adultery, we might as well be trying to put out a fire with diesel fuel.

Divorce. This is not God's answer to adultery. In Deuteronomy 24:1-4, divorce is dealt with on the basis of incompatibility or plain old dislike. But Jesus clarifies the issue completely by announcing divorce is not permitted except in cases of adulterous sexual immorality. In fact, in any case other than sexual adultery, He holds the person who asks for or forces a divorce responsible for the spouse as well as responsible for the person who enters a relationship with the innocent spouse. Stating that the person asking for a wrongful divorce causes their spouse to commit adultery, and anyone who marries them commits adultery as well. Strong words!

Oaths. Swearing on anything in heaven or on earth draws God to bear witness of the truth of the oath and whether we keep that oath. Therefore Jesus condemns the use of swearing by objects created or representative of Himself. Jesus concludes with a statement making shading or strengthening our promises based on an oath unnecessary and Christians should simply let yes or no be enough to cover their actions.

Personal Evaluation:

a. How long does it take for me to recognize that I am angry about something or at someone?

b. I agree or disagree with the amendment of:

Lesson 5
An Eye for an Eye; Love for an Enemy

Read Matthew 5:38-48.

1. What Old Testament law is Jesus amending and why?

2. How were the Pharisees misusing this Old Testament law for their own benefit?

3. What type of attack or wrong is Jesus describing in verse 39?

4. What is Jesus telling His disciples to do when wronged? Is He saying if they take out your eye give them the other? Explain.

5. How does verse 40 reveal the motives of some Pharisees and the way they used the Old Testament laws?

6. Describe how (in the times that Jesus was teaching) an evil or bad person might take advantage of an unsuspecting person.

7. Why does Jesus amend the Old Testament Law to the point of doing more than the Law requires?

8. How should we prepare ourselves to respond to insults, schemers, or evil-spirited people who try to take advantage of or harm us?

9. How has the love-your-neighbors-and-hate-your-enemies attitude affected our lives today?

10. The disciples have witnessed Jesus pray and miraculous blessings of strangers have resulted. What do you believe the disciples saw the purpose of prayer to be?

11. How do we pray for someone we love?

12. What must we do to be able to pray for our enemies or anyone who persecutes us for our faith?

13. How does Jesus describe the actions of a child of the Heavenly Father in verses 45-47?

14. Is it possible for us to be perfect? Explain.

15. What does Matthew 5:3 have to do with our perfection?

Commentary:

Jesus is amending the Levitical law found in Leviticus 24:20. The rule of thumb was that the punishment had to be at least as harsh as the crime, but it also limited the punishment never to exceed the crime. That's why it was written "an eye for an eye and a tooth for a tooth." The Pharisees misused this OT law to retaliate against those who might oppose them. This tactic caused great fear and even greater anger in the hearts of Israelite people.

In Matthew 5:39, Jesus describes this as a blatant insult whereby someone challenged another personally by slapping them with the back of their hand in the face, much like the old English gloves to the face was a challenge to a pistol duel to the death. Jesus is teaching the righteous response when we are wronged. The slap in the face would naturally provoke instant anger. We have already seen how Jesus views murder as a result of anger.

He uses strong analogies in this passage to demonstrate the strength it will take to respond in a way that is representative of the Kingdom. As people of God (His disciples) and heirs to the Kingdom of Heaven, we must always resist the desire to retaliate against even the harshest personal attacks. Jesus' extreme language indicates that when a Christian truly reflects the life of Christ, personal insults will come and our reaction to them will give evidence to His Spirit being in us.

In verse 40, we see that the Pharisees would literally try to sue the shirt off your back and use any possible means to do it, including twisting God's Old Testament Laws. They often would claim an offense, challenge the unsuspecting innocent party, and carry it as far as it took to get what they really wanted.

We see that Jesus amends the Old Testament Law to the point of doing more than the Law requires in order to reveal that righteousness can in no way be compared to human justice. Just doing what is required by human law is not a true reflection of kingdom righteousness.

Jesus' whole point is this: We must be prepared to respond to insults, schemers, or evil-spirited people who try to take advantage of us or even harm us before we find ourselves in the middle of one of these situations, always seeking ways to reveal the righteousness of Christ who lives in us. This is only possible when we expect these attacks to come and understand that this is what Jesus warns of in Matthew 5:10 when he teaches, "blessed are those who are persecuted for righteousness' sake for theirs is the kingdom of heaven." Instead of seeing every person who wrongs us as enemies, we need to realize the consequences of the love-your-neighbors-and hate-your-enemies attitude on our lives today. Hate has made us suspicious of all and paranoid even in the safety of our homes.

The disciples truly understood that when Jesus prayed, people were blessed. If they learned the secrets of prayer, they could experience the same result. God's will for our loved ones and our enemies alike will always result in Him being glorified. We should pray only for God to bless others in the way He desires to. We learn to pray for our enemies or anyone who persecutes us for our faith with a genuine desire that they be blessed the same way you desire your loved ones to be blessed. Jesus describes the actions of a child of the heavenly Father in Matthew 5:45-47 as not being limited to those in our family or our personal loved ones but, rather, includes strangers and enemies as well.

It is possible for us to be perfect but not in these bodies of sinful nature. However, it is possible to reflect the perfection of Christ in us by simply saying no to our natural desires and reactions and letting His desires and actions dictate our life responses. As He identifies in Matthew 5:3, realizing we are poor and cannot demonstrate perfection apart from Jesus Christ has everything to do with our perfection both now and in the eternal Kingdom.

Personal Evaluation:

a. I learned the following that challenged what I believe:

b. What can I do to change my reactions to negative attacks against me or my righteous stance?

Lesson 6
Giving to the Needy; Prayer and Fasting

Read Matthew 6:1-18.

1. How would you describe the right way and the wrong way to give to a needy person?

2. What comparisons do you see between verse 5 and verses 17-18?

3. What is Jesus telling His disciples not to do?

4. Why would a person pray outside but positioned in full view of those coming and going from the synagogue?

5. Why do some religions practice repetitive prayers or reciting prayers publicly?

6. Why do you believe Jesus teaches them to go into their room and close the door?

7. Do you believe this means that we should never pray publicly? Explain.

8. Why does Jesus say "this is how you should pray" rather than saying, "use these words and follow this prayer?"

9. Using only verses 7 and 8, how would you advise someone to pray?

10. List seven key aspects of the model prayer. (Look for the verbs, actions by God or man.)

11. What is the key to effective prayer seen in verses 14-15?

12. How would most Pharisees fast?

13. Describe a fast that Jesus says the Father will reward.

14. What verse in this passage tells us that Jesus expects us to fast?

15. Other than motives and recognition, what right method, or time for fasting does Jesus teach?

16. What would be the true purpose of fasting? Should it be a planned part of religious practice? Explain.

Commentary:
Jesus teaches that giving to the needy should be done the invisible way. Jesus makes it very clear that it is not the deed that is judged but rather the motive by which we are compelled that will be rewarded. When someone makes known their acts of charity, they have received all the reward their motives deserve regardless of how great or small men hold them in esteem.

One of the keys to effective Bible study is to recognize the repetition of words and discover what the repetitions emphasize. In the first 18 verses of Chapter 6, Jesus uses the word "Father" ten times. This should cause us to ask ourselves whether the Father is the focus of our prayers. Are our motives purely to bring glory to God the Father? As His children, do we really depend on Him for everything? Within the model prayer the word "forgive" is used six times and the instructions that follow clearly speak to the need for us to be right with all men and know that the sin of unforgiveness is not just a hindrance to our prayers. It is the answer to many unanswered prayers. God hates unforgiveness and we cannot expect to have a right relationship and be in communication with a forgiving God if we refuse to forgive others.

We must conclude that our deeds, prayers, or even fasting are private matters directly related to glorifying God the Father. Any other act is not an act of faith but rather an act for man's recognition and we in no way should expect the Lord to accept and reward acts performed for human acknowledgement.

Jesus teaches and expands our understanding of the prayer life to one that is like a private conversation between a child and his father. The Pharisees had made a practice of only praying when seen by the crowds and with lofty repetitious prayers recited from memory. Jesus identifies this as "prayers for the benefit of those hearing not at all meant solely for the ears of God." What Jesus is not saying is that prayer should only be done in private. We see Him gathering the disciples and praying with them on several occasions and we see the early church being built around regular prayer meetings.

The motive of our prayers causes God to listen or turn a deaf ear. Prayer is very simply talking with our heavenly Father through His Holy Spirit that lives in us in the name of the Son, Jesus Christ. If prayer is for any other reason or by any other method or name it goes unheard.

Matthew 6:7 is a very important reminder of praying out of duty or religious traditions. Using the term "empty phrases," Jesus is directing us to understand the sincerity of prayer. It is us talking with our Father, not chanting our desires to an unknown power out in the universe somewhere. Jesus clearly wants us to understand how to pray rather than what to pray. In fact, He gives us an outline for prayer that the Father hears. The prayer contains seven keys for us to follow:

- Worship and acknowledgement of God's Holy position
- Ask that the Kingdom be expanded
- Ask that God's will be done not ours
- Acknowledge God's sovereignty over all (in Heaven and on earth)
- Ask for your needs not your wants
- Ask for forgiveness and grace to forgive
- Ask for protection from the snares of Satan

The one predominate key to all effective prayer is outlined in verses 14 and 15. Jesus is proclaiming that a forgiving spirit, clear of guilt and at peace with our brothers, will be accepted. He also puts a huge emphasis on the fact that we are wasting our prayers to pray with unforgiveness toward others in our hearts.

Often the Pharisees would announce they were fasting to proclaim themselves to be more spiritual than others. Jesus, on the other hand, puts the emphasis on the importance of doing it for the glory of God, not the recognition of men.

In verse 16 and again in verse 17, Jesus leaves no doubt that we should fast by using the adverb "when." What Jesus does not teach is that fasting is abstaining from a particular thing or for a particular period of time. He leaves these methods to the dictates of man. Fasting as a corporate practice together or individually is not the point at all. The point is when we fast, we should never make a big deal of it nor draw attention to the fact that we are fasting.

God will judge our motives for fasting and our understanding of fasting will grow, not from the act or method, but rather from God's response to consecrated prayer that requires sustaining a sacrifice within the fast.

Personal Evaluation:

a. How does my prayer life need to change in order to match the instructions of Jesus?

b. What does a Godly fast look like for me personally?

Lesson 7
Treasures and Worry

Read Matthew 6:19-34.

1. Were any of the disciples wealthy enough to be storing money or material belongings? Explain.

2. Why doesn't Jesus simply say, "Forget about wealth. It's not for you?"

3. How do you believe Jesus views our financial success?

4. If the disciples did not have great possessions to store up, what is Jesus pointing to and why is this still relevant today?

5. Describe the mindset of a person that hides two million dollars' worth of gold in a box in their closet. How often do they think about the condition or safety of that gold?

6. What is the real choice Jesus is asking us to make in verses 19 and 20?

7. How would you answer Jesus if He asked, "What does your treasure in heaven look like and what are you going to do with your earthly treasures?"

8. How do the treasures we hold in our hearts change the way we view life, the way we act, and the way we express our belief in Christ?

9. How do we make money the enemy of God?

10. How does the teaching of treasures relate to worry?

11. What does verse 25 reveal about what the disciples were worried about?

12. Name two things that you worry most about.

13. Describe how you control the things that you worry about.

14. What does worry say about the disciples' faith and how does this relate to us?

15. Jesus asks, "And which of you by being anxious can add a single hour to his span of life?" So how can we use the previous teachings in this Sermon on the Mount as a recipe for overcoming worry?

16. What may or may not happen tomorrow?

7. What will change if you worry about it all day today?

> Commentary:
> The context of the sermon teaches us that these men have left everything to follow Jesus. Some of the disciples might have had advantageous jobs or prosperous businesses so, at the very least, they were jeopardizing their futures and, in reality, would have to start over from scratch. Maybe you have the question, "Is Jesus pointing to how others are using financial wealth to store up money and possessions or is He predicting the future of the disciples?"
>
> At no point do we see Jesus condemning wealth, or for that matter, advising the disciples on how to obtain wealth. This would suggest to us that Jesus expected them to have wealth in order to be in the position to decide what to do with their wealth. Surely some within the Christian family must have been accumulating material treasures. Jesus is pointing to the fact that all earthly treasures are subject to natural destruction or being stolen. We should also note that Jesus uses the pronoun "you"

("yourselves") throughout this teaching, suggesting that not only are earthly treasures individual and personal but so are Heavenly treasures.

We need to first recognize what a treasure is and what it is not. Treasures have one common thread. They are valuable to the holder. Each individual places value on people, places, or things. When we place such a high value on something that it consumes our thoughts and efforts to protect and even enhance it, then it has become a treasure.

Jesus is teaching that a Kingdom dweller (disciple of Christ) will place such a high value on eternal treasures that that will be what drives the disciple to use his or her life, monies, talents, and blessings to increase their heavenly treasures. However, when our hearts are consumed with temporary treasures, like money and material wealth, our source of light (Jesus/Heaven) is obscured. Soon our lives become dark and without eternal values. Things like money and possessions control our actions and we become consumed with protecting and increasing that which is temporary. When Christians are consumed with earthly treasures, they will find themselves at odds with God. Jesus points out that this will destroy our personal relationship with God.

A more prevalent problem that arises from having great treasures under our control is the problem of worry. Jesus starts this teaching with the statement, "Therefore…." What He is saying is that when we have a right perspective of treasures, worrying about the necessities of life should not be what defines us in the eyes of an on-looking world. Jesus then gives the recipe for righteous thinking concerning our needs and our treasures. "But seek first the kingdom of God and his righteousness, and all these things will be added to you." Everything He has taught previously in this sermon is teaching us how to seek the King's righteousness.

Personal Evaluation:

    a. I am concerned about personal possessions here on earth: (a) Very little (b) Some every day. (c) Several times a day. (d) All day. (e) All day every day.

    b. I personally accumulated treasures in the Kingdom of God by:

Personal Exercise:

Take one of your earthly possessions that is valuable to you and convert it into a heavenly treasure.

Lesson 8
Judging Others

Read Matthew 7:1-6.

1. What is significant about Jesus placing judgment of others directly after treasures and worries?

2. How do Christians who have rearranged their priorities to match Jesus' teachings tend to act as the judge over others who may still struggle with making Godly choices?

3. List some negative consequences of acting as the judge over other Christians.

4. What is the difference between being the judge and making sound judgments?

Read Matthew 7:3-6 and 7:15-20.

5. Is judgment necessary in order to "beware of false prophets?" Why or why not?

6. How do we use sound judgment without proclaiming judgment on other Christians?

7. What is significant about Jesus' use of extreme contrasts of a speck and a plank? Is it just as significant today?

8. Based on Matthew 7:3-5, describe your understanding of the right ways to use judgment.

Read Matthew 7:6.

9. Why is it more hypocritical for a Christian with a speck of fault to use the Bible as a tool to point out the faults of non-Christians than it is for a sinful non-Christian to speak against hypocritical Christians?

10. How should we use this teaching in relation to our judgments and interactions such as sharing the Gospel with sinful, uninterested people?

11. Does this verse teach us not to waste our time and God's Word on people we judge as sinful or does it teach us to judge something other than their sinfulness? Explain.

Commentary:
The context takes us to the theme of most of Jesus' teachings within this sermon. Our motives in making choices and the fact that we should stop trying to judge the motives of others are the primary points of this teaching. When we attempt to judge the heart of others, we are putting ourselves into the role of God for He alone knows the hearts of men apart from their actions. When we pronounce God-like judgments on other Christians, we assume the role of God, the judge, and we in turn will be held responsible for the actions we take against other believers.

One of the easiest traps for young Christians who have turned their lives, finances, and future over to God to fall into is the trap of judging other Christians and their motives. This is especially true in the area of how they use money. Jesus issues a stern warning for His disciples to not place themselves on the seat of supreme judge and think that their personal righteousness gives them the right to judge the intent and motive of others.

What Jesus is not teaching is an all-encompassing, "Judge not, that you not be judged." Teaching this is to take Matthew 7:1 completely out of the context of Scripture and ignore the many teachings of Christ on the correct methods of judging situations, circumstances, and disputes that affect the body of Christ. We only have to look a little deeper in this sermon to see where judgments are important to our being able to discern good, sound scriptural teaching from false, damaging teachings. But even in these judgments, we are first instructed to examine our own lives and motives. Instead of hunting for the tiniest mistake (speck) in the lives of others, we need to realize and deal with all personal sin, especially in the area of our motives. Deal with it like it was a plank in your eye obscuring your vision.

How this relates to sharing our faith, righteousness, and knowledge of Scripture with lost people is possibly the most unobserved teaching in the entire sermon. In verse 6, we see Jesus pointing to those who openly renounce God as well as the righteousness He is calling His disciples to. For the most part, He is referring to pagan Gentiles who reject all thought of worshiping the God of the Jews simply because they despise them. However, later in the Gospels we will see this same sentiment toward the

Pharisees who challenge Jesus' claims to be the divine Son of God. Jesus is clearly teaching that we should judge the actions of those who openly and contemptibly renounce the truth of the Gospel. Our message is not for the person whose choice is to not receive it regardless of the messenger. We have a responsibility to judge the actions of those we are sharing the Gospel with in the same way the Old Testament Law judges dogs and pigs as unclean animals. (See Matthew 7:6).

Personal Evaluation:

    a. What is in my life that causes me to judge the motives of other Christians?

    b. The following verses can help me to remember to take the plank out of my own eye:

Lesson 9
Ask, Seek and Knock & the Gates

Read Matthew 7:7–14.

1. Thinking inside the spiritual and eternal context of the sermon, to whom is Jesus making this promise? What is Jesus encouraging His disciples (then and now) to ask for?

2. What does the verb tense teach us to do if we ask and do not receive?

3. How intentional should we be in perusing this ask, seek, and knock promise? Who are we pursuing an answer from?

4. What does this pursuit of God do for our relationship with Him?

5. What one verse in the sermon helps you most in asking, seeking, and knocking?

6. What contrast does Jesus make in verse 11 between men and the Father in Heaven?

7. In verse 12, what does Jesus mean when He says, "So whatever you wish...?"

8. At the end of verse 12, Jesus concluded His teaching or amendments of the Old Testament law and completes Old Testament prophecy. If every believer were to understand and obey this one verse, list a few things that might change in this world.

9. Remember the context and describe the "narrow gate" in Matthew 7:13

10. How would you describe the contrasting "wide gate?"

11. How do sinful men receive eternal life?

12. How does this relate to verse 8?

13. How many other religions in the world today teach multiple ways to get eternal life?

Commentary:

The Bible teaches one way to eternal life–the small gate. World religions teach many ways to eternal life–the wide gate. Jesus has literally invited His disciples and us to live a supernatural life. We are from the very first point of the sermon taught that it is only possible when we are completely dependent upon Him. In these verses, He invites us to ask and keep on asking, to seek and keep on seeking, and to knock and keep on knocking. Unless this instruction is understood within the context of the sermon, one might tend to believe a Christian can ask for anything and everything and receive it. Not!

It is all about the righteous relationship between us, as God's children, and Him, as the sovereign Lord of our lives, and our asking, seeking and knocking for His will to be done in our lives here and now just as it is each and every moment in heaven. There is a very important reason that prayer is positioned right in the middle of the text. Every right relationship is dependent on good communication, and our righteous prayer life is the key to the Christian's life in Christ. The one unmistakable verse of instruction concerning intimate prayer is found in Matt. 6:6: "But when you pray, go into your room and shut the door and pray to your Father who is in secret. And your Father who sees in secret will reward you."

Jesus does not condemn public prayer. However, we do not carry on intimate human conversations in public before an audience. Our intimate conversation with God is to be as private as a closed-door conversation between a parent and their child.

Allowing the context to rule, we come to the conclusion that when we ask, seek, and knock for what is in line with God's Kingdom and righteous will taught within the sermon, we have the greatest promise a child can have. Our promise is unconditional love, provision, and communion with the almighty Creator of the universe. The greatest part is we will have it according to how we would want it!

The sad but very real truth is few will ever truly pursue the righteous relationship with God. We live in a world that is under the influence of Satan. All his shiny things that distract us from the eternal Kingdom become the objects of our desires and passions and, in the process, our relationship with a Holy Father is lost. We literally choose the temporary pleasures of the day over an eternal relationship with God that is developed through intimate personal contact and righteous living here and now. The Golden Rule is simply an outward result of a right relationship with a generous and loving Father.

Personal Evaluation:

    a. As I look at my life today I can see that I need to be more dependent on God in the areas of:

    b. In order to have a greater more intimate relationship with God, I will begin today to:

Lesson 10
The Tree and Its Fruit
The Wise and Foolish Builder

Read Matthew 7:15–27.

1. What are some of the fruits of a false prophet?

2. Jesus points out that it is easy to identify a bad person (tree) and just as easy to identify a good person (tree). But what about a wolf in sheep's clothing? Who is He talking about here?

3. How does verse 21 help us to identify the wolves?

4. Which one of the disciples could be identified with verses 22-23?

5. How does the statement "many will say to me, Lord, Lord" reflect on Christianity today?

6. How can we determine if a person's good works are of God or false?

7. What should our response be when we encounter people doing good deeds or ministries to glorify themselves or for personal gain?

Read Matthew 5:24–27.

1. How would you describe these verses as they apply to the purpose for Jesus teaching these truths to His disciples and to us?

Commentary:
In Matthew 5:15-27, Jesus is definitely pointing out that devoted followers (disciples) must be prepared to recognize those who come in the name of Jesus but actually are false prophets (preachers) that advocate the wide and easy road. They will look godly but preach in contradiction to the righteous will of God we have studied throughout this sermon. They will use these righteous truths but water them down until, like C. H. Spurgeon says, "they don't have enough truth to make a single bowl of soup for a sick grasshopper."

When Christians are either immature and have not been taught the truths of this sermon or they have little knowledge and lose their dependent spirit, they are susceptible to these false teachers who talk a good talk and sound like godly teachers. In truth, they are teaching something that resembles truth but leads people to a different source than complete dependence on Christ and His Holy Spirit. When Jesus begins to speak to the character of false preachers, He does not say, "Make sure what they teach follows these teachings of mine." Instead, He tells us to look at their fruit. In other words, if the lives and righteousness of those who follow or sit under the teaching of these false teachers do not match this sermon, then it is apparent that the fruit produced is something other than the righteous life Jesus wants for His followers.

Jesus places an extreme emphasis here on those who falsely claim Jesus as their Lord. He once again points to their lives and says if they do not do the will of God, they cannot be of God. Even on the Day of Judgment, they will claim to Jesus Himself that their works and teachings were in His name. Surely Jesus, who knows every man's heart, will expose their deeds and teachings, fruits and followers. Surely, as He announces here, He will send them to eternal hell.

It is not enough for us just to hear or even study these truths of the Sermon on the Mount. We must be obedient to each teaching found there and our spiritual lives must fully and completely be dependent and founded in Christ or we will be like the house built on sandy soil. We will struggle to understand this Christian life and a spiritual fall is immanent.

Personal Evaluation and Exercise:

Discover who is on the narrow road. Make a point to ask three different trusted Christian friends (not family members) each of the following four questions. On a separate piece of paper record the short version of their answers. This is not an exercise to educate other. It is an opportunity to learn how many people have heard Jesus' teaching in the Sermon on the Mount and confirm whether or not you are on the narrow road.

a. Which of the beatitudes found in the Sermon on the Mount do you believe is the most important in order for us to understand what pleases God and why?

b. How often do you have discussions about sharing your faith with other Christians?

c. Have your ever studied the consequences of adultery, divorce, or wrongly condemning other believers?

d. How does Jesus teach us to build our house on solid rock?

"Everyone who hears these words of mine and does them will be like a wise man who built his house on the ROCK"
~Jesus of Nazareth

PART 3

A Disciple's View of
Evangelism

*"Go into all the world and proclaim the gospel
to the whole creation"
~Jesus
(Mark 16:15)*

Building an Evangelical Foundation

Complete assurance of your salvation and a personal relationship with Jesus Christ is the only valid prerequisite to committing one's life to being a disciple maker. Disciples, much like men and women who have enlisted in the military, surrender all personal rights to their commander. A disciple is to the person of Jesus Christ as a soldier is to an officer. If we are not fully surrendered to the Lordship of Jesus Christ, our will, at some point, will circumvent the Will of God, causing us to become self-centered Christians. We will find ourselves leading others to follow our will instead of surrendering to the leadership of the Holy Spirit.

Jesus teaches us in Matthew 5:15 not to hide our light under a basket but rather to set it on a pedestal for all men to see and be drawn to it. The first step to letting our light shine is to understand what we believe and why. Every disciple needs to form their own understanding of the Gospel and be able to communicate it in a very easy way to others, whether they are Christians or people who have never heard the Gospel before.

Although the Gospel is identified clearly in the Scriptures and should always be based upon Scripture, we need to form our own ability to communicate the Gospel of Jesus in a way that doesn't come across like a preacher preaching from a pulpit. Nor should we do it in a way that sounds like we are trying to force the person to believe what we believe simply because we are passionate about it. Communicating the Gospel should always be personal to us. In other words, it should always include our personal story, what brought us to a decision of believing it, and how the Gospel has changed the way we think, the way we act, the way we live our lives and the choices that we make.

As we share the Gospel, we should always present a clear personal choice. Lead them to answer this question: "Is Jesus truly Lord of my life?" It is not necessary for a disciple offering the perfect gift of God's grace to feel the duty to convict another by telling them if they don't believe and pray a prayer they are headed to hell. Simply present the truth entwined with your personal story and lead them to answer the question personally, "Do I truly believe Jesus is God and am I willing to surrender my will and desire to Him as Lord of my life?" (See 2 Corinthians 5:15.)

Our ability to share the Gospel never relies upon our own intellect but rather must always rely upon the Holy Spirit. Our fine speech or our ability to communicate in excellent ways never trumps the Spirit's power to draw a person to the point of conviction that leads to personal salvation. (See John 3:31-36.)

For this study to be an effective tool to our growth as disciples, we must begin to **practice two very important aspects** of evangelism that are seldom taught and even avoided by many Christians.

    1. Talk with other Christians about our personal relationship with Christ and the Gospel. Instead of starting a conversation about sports, business, politics or even religion, make it a habit to start conversations by asking questions about sharing the Gospel or ways to approach non-Christians with the Gospel. Share your recent experiences in sharing your faith and ask them what they think about this.

2. Form the habit of including comments or phrases within your everyday conversations that announce you are a Christian to strangers or people who obviously are not Christians. Use simple phrases like "praise the Lord," "thank God," "amazing God," "God outdid Himself today," "God is good," "I am so blessed," "if that's what God wants," and any other words or phrases that identify you with God's people. You can use song lyrics, prayers and even verses of Scripture. (**Warning:** Avoid using church language that sends alarms and causes many lost people to throw up a red flag and run away. Examples: testimony, saved, gospel, evangelize, the lost, believers and membership.)

Have you ever known a Christian who was consistently effective in sharing his or her faith with a stranger without ever having learned a single verse or studied God's plan as it's laid out in Scripture? How about a Christian who shares the Gospel with the intent to educate the lost person about the whole Bible?

Once, while serving on mission in Brazil, a young man on the team was sharing his faith with a young mother through a translator. He began by describing the Genesis account of creation and for an hour he went step-by-step through the Bible until he reached Revelation 3:20 where he quoted the verse and asked the woman, "Are you willing to open the door of your heart and let Jesus in?" With a bewildered look on her face, and after an awkward pause, she replied, "Do you know Michael Jackson?" That's a funny but true story that we can all learn from.

Most Christians never share their faith because of a basic fear that the person will reject or misunderstand because we don't know enough Scripture or because we will flat out not be able to put it into words. Our faith can, and even should be, at the heart of every conversation we have. I am not suggesting we should never talk about sports, fashions, or politics, but when we start our conversations with a subject that is disconnected from our faith; we will seldom if ever get the conversation to a place where we can share our faith. This is especially true in a setting where we are talking with strangers who may have never heard the Gospel. However, it is just as true, and probably more critical, that we learn to talk with other Christians about the Gospel and ways to share our faith with others.

Over the course of this study, we will define and build a personal foundation for sharing the Gospel. This study, unlike many that teach a presentation or method, is not intended to give you a cookie-cutter way to share or cold call. Instead, it is a guide to building a personal foundation to sharing our faith. We must become comfortable with who we are as Disciples of Christ and be able to lead others to the basic truth of the Gospel and the foundation of our faith.

Before you start, please prayerfully consider whether or not you are committed to use what you learn to build your personal foundation, and make sharing your faith in Jesus with others the point of your life.

Step 1:

Sharing the Gospel in Your Own Words

Use the spaces below the questions to record your answers. This will give you an opportunity to put into words what the Gospel is to you at this stage in your life as a disciple.

1. Explain the Gospel in your own words.

2. How would you explain sin to a person who has never heard the Gospel?

3. What would your answer be to the person who asks, "What is this salvation that you're talking about?"

4. How would you describe your personal relationship with Jesus Christ to a person who wants to know about it but has no clue as to what it means to him or her?

5. What Scriptures have you used to form your way of sharing the Gospel?

Read 1 John 5:9-13.

6. According to verses 11 and 12, describe the Spirit of God's version of the Gospel.

Read Romans 4:13 through 5:21. Answer the following questions about sin.

7. How would you use these verses to explain why all men are born sinners?

8. Why is understanding Abraham's faith so important for us to overcome our sinful nature?

9. Describe the contrasting difference between the reign of sin and the reign of grace.

10. What are some key verses in this passage that help us to form our foundational understanding of the Gospel?

11. Is it all that important to point out that someone is a sinner or should we simply assume they know they are a sinner and move on? Explain.

Commentary:

Most of us will go a lifetime without encountering a single person who does not admit he or she is a sinner. However, it's the one time that we do that leads us to prepare to share the truth that all men have sinned. (See Romans 3:23.) The truth is that Jesus only pointed out and condemned sin. We never see Him attacking or belittling the sinful person.

We will surely encounter many obvious sinners and our human reaction will be to judge the person. We must remind ourselves that it is only by God's grace that we are forgiven of our sins and justified. At the same time, we must guard against being tolerant or apathetic of any sin. We often see Jesus deliberately pointing out a person's sins for the purpose of helping them understand the consequences of sin and His free gift of eternal life.

Read Romans 6 to gain a clear understanding, particularly of verse 23.

12. How would you see yourself using a verse like Romans 6:23 as you share the Gospel?

It is easy to get hung up on pointing out sin and that we all are sinners while at the same time sounding like we are above sin as well as better than the person we may be talking with. However, Jesus never offered a human solution to our sin nature but, rather, He offered forgiveness and a restored relationship. As disciples, we should not ask unbelievers to take a blind leap of faith. Rather, we extend God's gift and we lead those who receive the gift into a complete understanding of what Jesus teaches. This is where relating the Gospel to our personal experience becomes critical. If we are to carry someone into a relationship with Jesus, they need to believe we are in it with them.

13. How would you describe God's plan to redeem the world to a person that recognizes he is a sinner and lost?

14. If you had to narrow this plan or truth to one verse of Scripture, which would you choose?

> We always need to lead the person to understand the choices they have, as well as the consequences of the wrong choice. We must not lead people to believe that merely acknowledging that Jesus is the Son of God and the Savior of mankind is sufficient to equal salvation from eternal death. We must bring every non-believer to a point of making a decision. Even if we do not witness the person surrender his or her life to Christ, we must at the very least plant the understanding that God requires his or her conscious choice.

Read Romans 10:9-13.

15. Break this passage down and explain the choices and actions we all must make and explain how you would emphasize the importance of Jesus being Lord as it applies to salvation.

It is critical that everyone who puts their faith in Christ Jesus understand they have the assurance of eternal life. Disciples do not doubt or hang on a promise that is only good until we sin again.

Read John 5:24 and reread 1 John 5:11-13.

16. How would you use these verses to describe assurance of salvation to someone who just put their faith in Jesus?

One of the primary reasons Christians give for not sharing their faith is that they do not believe they know enough Scripture. In other words, they have not, or believe they cannot, memorize Scripture. Many Christians are intimidated by memorizing Scripture and even more intimidated by someone who has memorized a lot of Scripture. If this is true about Christians, just think what it might be to someone who is unfamiliar with Scripture altogether.

When we quote Scripture to a lost person, we need to be mindful of how they hear the Word of God, and know that it is very easy to come across as a self-righteous religion pusher rather than one concerned for them and their eternal destination. We must discipline ourselves to trust the Holy Spirit to bring to our remembrance what we have committed to memory.

17. From what we have studied so far, list five key verses that you feel will help you form a foundation to sharing the Gospel more easily, and behind each verse, describe the role each verse will play in explaining the Gospel.

Step 2:

Incorporating Our Story

Often, we tend to share what is known as our "testimony," but it seldom tells the real story of what God has done to change our hearts and lives. However, if we will learn to share our story as it matches up with the Gospel, it becomes a part of the Gospel and people can see themselves in our shoes. Everyone needs a savior, but sometimes the Gospel appears too easy and we come across as selling our beliefs.

Our story should have three parts and each part should be told in honesty and truth as if we were talking to our grandmother who knows everything about us.

1. Who were you **before you gave your life to Christ?** Sin does not have to be detailed, but simply giving the canned "I was a sinner" testimony will be seen as fake. Sharing your hurts and struggles will cause someone to identify with you.

2. What was it that caused you to realize you needed to **surrender your life and let Jesus be Lord**? Many are able to communicate that they realized they were sinners and accepted God's forgiveness, but few are able to verbalize how repentance came to their lives and what that looked like. In other words, when did you give up and let Jesus be Lord?

3. What does your **personal relationship with Christ** look like today? How has God shown you His love and how has Jesus revealed Himself in your life, as well as the assurance of salvation that brings eternal peace to your heart?

The goal of this section is to help us incorporate the scriptural context of the Gospel into our personal story.

1. What Scriptures identify you as a sinner and subsequently help the one you're speaking with see himself as a sinner as well?

2. Use your Scriptures and describe in your own words how you felt when you realized your life was headed away from God and you, like all men, are a sinner.

3. What Scriptures helped you realize Jesus was the answer and you needed a Savior?

4. Use your Scriptures and describe, in your own words, how these Scriptures brought you to the realization, that without Christ as your Lord, you were hopelessly separated from the love of God.

5. What Scriptures give you faith in the fact that you are in an eternal relationship with God and you are now one of His children?

6. Use these Scriptures to describe your life today and what it is like to have a personal relationship with Christ.

Step 3:

Preparing to Share Our Faith

We should have at least five basic Scriptures to follow and guide us through the Gospel. We should also have a clear understanding of how our life stories fit within the truths of the Gospel. The Gospel of Jesus Christ is truth, period. Our stories confirm the Gospel as true to all we proclaim it to. To effectively proclaim the truth of the Gospel and who we are in Christ, we will need to memorize these key verses.

Memorization only works if you do it every day, several times a day. An accountability partner is a great way to force you to do it every day. The partners must be true to each other and to Jesus. We are going to learn that knowing the address of the verse is more important than being able to quote the verse word for word. It's a proven fact that people retain much more when they read something themselves rather than it being told or having it recited to them. It also helps to write out the verse.

Using the following memory verses as a guide, start at your own pace and learn to memorize through consistent practice. Memorize, in order, the address of the passage, the verse itself, and then repeat the address. I suggest that you purchase from NavPress the Navigators memory tool called Topical Memory System. Begin to recite the verses to yourself until you feel you can recite them by memory to your partner. Do not hesitate to call your partner, who should be doing the same, and recite your verses from memory. Continue reciting the verse even if you feel you have it down and add another verse. Continue this practice for 10 weeks and you will discover the joy of having God's Word sharp and fully committed to memory.

Sin: Romans 3:23

Consequences of Sin: Romans 6:23

God's Love/Gift: Romans 5:8

Salvation: Romans 10:9-10

Assurance: John 5:24

Time to Practice:

With a partner playing the role of an interested lost person, share the Gospel. When you are through we will review together what you think about the exercise. Write down and record any areas on which you need to concentrate on and improve.

Step 4:

Conversations with Christians

The Bible gives us examples of how Christians interacted in the church, so let's **read Acts 4:31-35.**

1. Is boldness one of the gifts of the Holy Spirit or is the courage to speak boldly an evidential attribute of the Holy Spirit living in us? Explain your answer.

2. In the early church, do you believe conversations about sports, politics, business, the weather, or maybe the latest Christian arrested for sharing Jesus dominated the Sunday morning Bible study hour? What kind of conversations between Christians led to the selling of property and possessions to meet the needs of all?

Read Acts 9:26-31.

3. Have you ever brought an obviously sinful person into a fellowship of believers for the purpose of introducing them as your Christian brother or sister in Christ? What motivated Barnabas to risk his position in the Jerusalem Church?

4. Do you believe this type of event took place often in New Testament Church?

5. What is more common in the church today?:
   a. sharing our faith with a stranger and never seeing them again
   b. sharing our faith with a stranger, seeing them surrender to Christ, and bringing them to church and introducing him or her as our new brother or sister.

6. What keeps us from drawing sinners into our church relationships today?

7. What actions can we take together to overcome this void?

Read John 4:1–11.

8. Jesus is about to change this woman's eternal destiny. What can we learn from His conversation that we might be able to use as we approach strangers?

9. How would you start a conversation with someone that either you might have prejudices against or who might have prejudices against you?

10. How would you approach a friend with the Gospel?

11. What can make you more confident and comfortable about sharing your faith?

Study the following well known methods of sharing the Gospel message. Keep in mind that we must take these as building blocks. Even if one of these sounds perfect for you, it must still be adapted into the way you talk and become a natural part of your conversations.

Do not make the mistake of memorizing one of these and learning to recite it. It will come off as a canned presentation to the listener. This can also cause us to become dependent on it and create boundaries that end up controlling every aspect of how we share the Gospel. Remember, the goal is to make a disciple of Christ (draw another into a relationship with Christ) and not to simply get a person to agree with your beliefs or say a sinner's prayer. When we share our faith in the right way, we never stop growing in the use of God's Word, learning from our experiences, and we never stop making disciples.

William Fay's Share Jesus without Fear

Step One: Use Questions That Determine Where God is Working

    1. Do you have any kind of spiritual belief?

    2. Who is Jesus to you?

    3. Do you believe there is a heaven and a hell?

    4. If you died right now, where would you go? If heaven, why?

    5. If what you believe were not true, would you want to know it?

If yes, open Bible

If no, do nothing.

Step Two: Let the Bible Speak

Read each verse out loud and ask, "What does this verse say to you?

    1. Romans 3:23: All have sinned.

    2. Romans 6:23: The wages of sin is death.

    3. John 3:3: You must be born again. Ask: "Why did Jesus come to die?

    4. John 14:6: I am the Way.

    5. Romans 10:9-11: If you confess… you will be saved.

    6. 2 Corinthians 5:15: No longer live for themselves.

    7. Revelation 3:20: I stand at the door and knock.

Step Three: Close with Key Questions

    1. Are you a sinner?

    2. Do you want forgiveness for your sins?

    3. Do you believe Jesus died on the cross?

    4. Are you willing to surrender your life to Christ?

    5. Are you ready to invite Jesus into your life and into your heart?

Step Four: Be Silent and Pray

"Heavenly Father, I have sinned against You. I want forgiveness for all my sins. I believe that Jesus died on the cross for me and rose again. Father, I give You my life to do with as You wish. I want Jesus Christ to come into my life and into my heart. Amen."

Principle

Success in witnessing is living the Christian life day-by-day, sharing the gospel, and trusting God for the results. Success is not bringing someone to Christ. God does the work. We cannot fail. It is all God's work.

Truths

"For by grace you have been saved through faith. And this is not your own doing; it is the gift of God...." (Eph. 2:8)

"And I was with you in weakness and in fear and much trembling, and my speech and my message were not in plausible words of wisdom, but in demonstration of the Spirit and of power." (1 Cor. 2:3-4)

"No one can come to me unless it is granted him by the Father." (John 6:65)

"Therefore, we are ambassadors for Christ, God making his appeal through us." (2 Corinthians 5:20)

ABC's of Salvation

A. Admit to God that you have sinned and disobeyed Him.

Romans 3:23: "...for all have sinned and fall short of the glory of God..."

B. Believe that Jesus died on the cross and rose again. His blood was shed to pay for your sin.

John 3:16: "For God so loved the world, that He gave His only Son, that whoever believes in Him should not perish but have eternal life

Jesus took the punishment for you.

C. Confess that Jesus can forgive you of your sins.

Romans 10:13 "...everyone who calls on the name of the Lord will be saved."

If you need help praying, the following prayer will help you.

Dear Lord Jesus,

 I admit that I am a sinner and I am in need of Your forgiveness. I want to turn from my sins and follow You. I believe that You are the Son of God who died on the cross for me and my sins. You were buried, rose to life again and You are coming back. I accept the gift of eternal life through faith and belief in You alone. I receive You as Lord and Savior. In Jesus' Name, Amen.

The Bridge to Life
By The Navigators

One of the oldest questions humankind has been asking is, "How can I know God?" The question is a valid one. What is He like? What can we do to please Him? How can we get to Heaven? If we work hard enough to be a good enough person will He accept us then? If we do enough religious activities to get His attention, will that do it?

Fortunately for us, the answer is surprisingly simple. The "Gospel" that the Bible talks about literally means, "The Good News," and the news is good indeed!

MAN & GOD

First, we have to start at the beginning. In Genesis 1:26, when God created the first humans, He said, "Let us make mankind in our image, in our likeness", then God blessed them and spent the days walking and talking with the people He had created. In short, life was good.

MAN	GOD
SIN	HOLY

But why isn't life like that anymore? What happened to mess everything up? This brings us to the second point: when we (humankind) chose to do the opposite of what God told us, sin poisoned the world. Sin separated us from God, and everything changed. Romans 3:23 says, "For all have sinned and fall short of the glory of God," and in Isaiah 59:2 we're told, "your iniquities have separated you from your God; your sins have hidden his face from you so that he will not hear." This is especially bad news because there is no way for us to get across that gap on our own. We (humankind) have tried to find our way back to God and a perfect world on our own ever since then, and without any luck. We try to get there by being good people, or through religion, money, morality, philosophy,

115

education, or any number of other ways, but eventually we find out that none of it works. "There is a way that seems right to a man, but in the end it leads to death" (Proverbs 14:12).

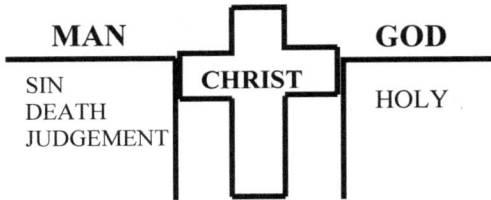

MAN   **CHRIST**   **GOD**

SIN   HOLY
DEATH
JUDGEMENT

There is only one way to find peace with God, and the Bible says it is through Jesus Christ. We were stranded without any way of getting back to our Creator, and we needed a way to pay for our sins and be clean again so that we could be welcomed back to be with Him. Romans 5:8 says, "But God demonstrates His own love for us in this: While we were still sinners, Christ died for us." So this is the Good News—that even though we were still enemies of God (as one translation says), Jesus came to die on the cross and pay the price for our sins so that we could have a relationship with Him again. John 3:16 says, "For God so loved the world that He gave His one and only son, that whoever believes in Him shall not perish but have eternal life."

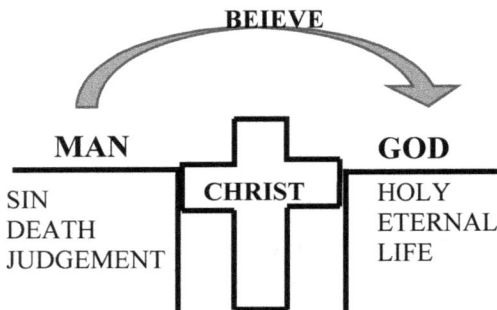

BEIEVE

MAN   **CHRIST**   **GOD**

SIN   HOLY
DEATH   ETERNAL
JUDGEMENT   LIFE

What then should be our reaction to this awesome news? This brings us to the last and most important part. John 5:24 says, "I tell you the truth, whoever hears my word and believes Him who sent me has eternal life and will not be condemned; he has crossed over from death to life." Jesus Christ himself even says, "I have come that they may have life, and have it to the full" (John 10:10), and Romans

116

5:1 says, "We have peace with God through our Lord Jesus Christ."
So how can I have peace with God, life to the full, and be confident of eternal life like these verses say? First, through an honest prayer to God, I have to admit that I'm not perfect—that I can't escape my sins, and I can't save myself. I follow this admission by believing that Jesus Christ died for me on the cross and rose from the grave, conquering death and sin. Then I invite Jesus Christ to live in me and be the Lord of my life, accepting His free gift of eternal life with Him.

The prayer can go something like this:

"Dear Jesus,
I know that I am a sinner and that I need You to forgive me. I know that You died a painful death so that my sins could be washed clean. Thank you. I want to make You the Lord of my life, and I will trust and follow You. Everything I have is Yours now.
In Your name, Lord.
Amen."

There is nothing magical about these words. It's not the words themselves that make things right between you and God—it's whether or not your heart really means it. We know this because in 1 Samuel 16:7, the Bible says, "The Lord does not look at the things people look at. People look at the outward appearance, but the Lord looks at the heart."
The best part of this whole process is that it doesn't matter how badly we've messed up, Jesus is powerful enough to save anyone from their sins—even the worst of us. Romans 10:13 says, "Everyone who calls on the name of the Lord will be saved." That's fantastic news—no matter how badly we've messed up, we can place our complete trust in Jesus, and He will wipe all of our sins off the face of the earth. Jesus is the bridge to life.

12. Can you identify the one missing element in each of these methods?

13. Can you see yourself using one or all of these methods? How would you change or adjust them to fit what gives you confidence?

Step 5:

Building Your Own Foundation

The _____ Method.

(Write your name in the space)

1. Identify a few Scriptures, ones you have in memory, that you can easily recall and that will help someone clearly understand God's plan for his or her salvation. At this point, add a topic to your verses to help you place the Scripture in context of your personal story. For instance, "all sin." (Romans 3:23).

2. Using the topics and the three parts to your personal story, along with your memorized Scriptures, write out how you would share your faith and the Gospel. Use your personal story and memorized Scripture.

Practical Exercises:

a. Being able to comfortably talk with other Christians about our faith should and can be a natural part of our relationships at church or wherever we encounter brothers and sisters in Christ. However, we must not assume it will happen naturally. Most Christians, even those who grew up in church, have not grown up with the practice of talking about faith and faith-sharing encounters with each other. Getting started will not be easy. For that reason, we should first build our own confidence with the Christians we are most familiar with and test the waters, so to speak.

b. Once you pick whom you will share with, don't set prerequisites for how the conversation will go. As a matter of fact, just jump into it with both feet in hopes that it will shock them into a natural response. Don't be surprised if they stare at you like a calf looking at a new gate. It is also important not to form the habit of approaching a friend in the same way each time you share an evangelistic experience.

c. It is okay to be creative. One of my favorite ways to share an evangelistic experience with brothers is to start with the statement, "I went fishing this week." Then I share how I shared the Gospel or went out to evangelize in public. At first you may have to start by simply asking questions like, "What do you think about someone sharing their faith this way?"

d. How do you see yourself starting a conversation about an evangelism experience with another Christian? List as many conversation starters or questions as you can.

e. Using one of your conversation starters or questions, approach a Christian friend and start a conversation about an evangelistic experience.

Journal your conversation here:

Step 6:

Sharing Your Faith with Non-Christians

Beginning to share with strangers that you are not sure about and those you know are not Christians requires a similar attitude but an entirely different approach. Jesus gave us the example in John 4 with the Samaritan woman. Somehow we must draw others into a conversation. Jesus did it with a request for something that only required she use her ladle. Maybe we need to learn to ask questions that bond us to the person.

With any first encounter, we need to build a trust factor as quickly as possible. In the situation with this woman, Jesus took her slightly prejudicial response and turned it into an offering of something only He could give her. What is interesting is how quickly He moved to this offer of living water. We need to heed this example. Building a bond of trust can take place in as little as the first few seconds and we should never make building a trust bond our priority. If we do, we will soon learn just how hard it is to get around to sharing the Gospel.

I am sure Jesus was thirsty, but it is obvious He was not as thirsty as the story makes it sound. Do we ever see her giving Him a drink? Maybe the question was intended for you and me as much as it was for her. What I mean is Jesus saw what she had come to the well with as well as what she came for and He used that to start the conversation. We should observe what others are up to, such as who they work for, what kind of work they do, what they drive, even what they are eating, and form an inquisitive question to get the conversation started as well as to indicate "It's okay to talk with me."

Jesus broke a prejudicial rule that Jews did not speak to Samaritans. This drew the woman to respond as well as to trust Him enough to enter into a conversation and ask a personal question. Jesus never waivers from His goal and the result was her conversion recorded in eternal history.

Over the next few weeks, we will work in teams to begin to make sharing our faith with strangers and the lost a part of who we are and what we love to do. It is important to record these events. God will continually teach us about Himself and draw us deeper into a personal relationship through each and every one of these encounters with lost strangers. Journaling our experiences will permit us to evaluate our evangelism efforts.

I shared my faith with _____.
(Journal here or on a separate piece of paper if you need more space.)

I shared my faith with _____.

I shared my faith with _____.

I shared my faith with _____.

PART 4

Go Make
Disciples

---

*"If anyone would come after me, let him deny himself and take up his cross
daily and follow me."*
~Jesus
(Luke 9:23)

I am a Disciple Maker!

In Part 4 we will discover that Jesus has already laid out the plan and allows us to see his strategy of making disciple and use that as the pattern for building our own individual and corporate strategy and plan. Once we see ourselves as disciple makers we will then take all that we have learned and build a strategy and a plan for us to use in going and making disciples.

Read John 14.

1. As you read this chapter, do you believe Jesus was making things up as He went along or did He have a strategy, a plan, or directions to follow? Explain.

2. In verses 10 and 11, how does Jesus describe the relationship with the Father? How does this work?

3. Describe the promise in verse 12 as it applies to us here and now.

4. What is the purpose of Jesus' work in and through us?

Very carefully re-read John 14:12-20.

5. What is God's promise to all believers?

6. It is hard to imagine being able to do greater works than Jesus. Notice that the fact Jesus states in verse 12 is not a part of the later promise in verse 14. When you read this passage in context, how does the promise found in verses16 through 20 relate to the promise found in verses 13 and 14?

7. What is the key to the disciples' successful works found right in the middle of this passage?

8. Jesus points to His works as evidence that proves He and the Father are one. How would you as a disciple give evidence that you and Jesus are one?

9. According to John 14:21 and again in John 15:10, Jesus is our example and He tells us He was completely obedient to His father, so much so that they walked this earth as one. Would it be fair to say that if we want to know the power of God, the love of God, the presence of God, we must be completely obedient to the Word of God, to the commands of Jesus, and to the guidance and prompting of the Holy Spirit?

Read John 15:12 & 17.

10. Pay close attention to commandment found here, then, in your own words, write out what this means to you personally.

11. How critical is obedience to this command, to our personal relationship with Jesus/God?

Read Matthew 28:18-20.

12. How does this command fit into your personal relationship with Jesus?

13. How do you expect God to respond and how will it affect our relationship with Christ if we ignore this command or make excuses to avoid being obedient to it?

14. What is God's personal promise to those who are obedient to go and make disciples?

Personal Evaluation:

   a. I do understand what it takes to be a true disciple of Christ and because of that I am prepared to make disciples. I believe the best way for me personally to make disciples is to:

Building a Strategic Plan to Make Disciples

Making disciples is not easy and it only happens when the Holy Spirit is at work in both the student and the teacher's life. Men have made disciple making something very different than Jesus teaches in the Gospels. It is important for us to be aware of how Satan will attempt to stop the disciple maker before they ever starts and at every step of this process. Let's start by looking at **five myths (or Satan's lies)** that keep us from ever attempting to make disciples:

1. **We need to gather a group.** For some reason we have taken the plural term "disciples" in Jesus' commission to "go and make disciples" to mean we must form groups of Christians to meet corporately before we can be successful at making disciples.

2. **We need a more educated person to join in our efforts before we attempt to make a disciple.** We must not forget that making disciples is all about leading believers to understand and have a greater relationship with Christ and not about religious education. The time will come when we need to recognize we have grown the disciple all we can and it is at that point we will need the more educated disciple makers help.

3. **We can make disciples on Sunday morning.** The idea that we can make ourselves available for one hour on Sunday morning and somehow lead others into a daily relationship is contradictory to God's Word and the examples set by Christ in the Gospels.

4. **Disciple makers will be judged by a harsher or greater standard than other believers.** Judgment and the Law were never meant to control the children of God through instilling great fear in them. They are, on the other hand, intended to give believers a healthy dose of fearful respect for the One who can send a man to hell. Ask yourself this: Who is under greater judgment? The believer who hears the command to make disciples but never does or the one that attempts to do so out of obedience to the One that commands him?

5. **Making disciples requires me to be a great soul winner and lead many people to salvation.** Jesus said, "No one can come to me unless the Father who sent me draws them." So we have no reason to put undue pressure on ourselves. Counting numbers is an ego thing unique to men. Sharing the One we love is something we do because we love not in order to prove our love. Going and making disciples starts by sharing the Gospel of Jesus Christ. But if we stop there, we are no more obedient than if we ignore the command all together.

Keys to Establishing a Strategic Plan to Make Disciples

1. And he said the them, "Follow me, and I will make you fishers of men." (Matthew. 4:19) We must learn to invite other believers to become disciples. Jesus did not wait for men to show up at His doorstep or approach Him in the temple. He was out on the roads going about His daily endeavors.

2. He said to them, "Come and you will see." So they came and saw where he was staying…" (John 1:39) We must be willing to invest time and energy, and open our lives to potential disciples. Jesus never invited the disciples to meet Him at a certain place for a short lesson. Rather, He literally invested His life in the disciples.

3. "Truly, truly, I say to you, unless one is born again he cannot see the kingdom of God." (John 3:3) We must lead people to recognize their own salvation. Recognizing our spiritual birth should be as evident as looking out the window and telling if the wind is blowing or not.

4. "Truly I say to you, unless you turn and become like children you will never enter the kingdom of heaven." (Matthew 18:3) We must teach other believers how to have a child-to-father understanding in order to maintain a right relationship with Christ.

5. "And the rain fell, and the floods came, and the winds blew and beat on that house, but it did not fall, because it had been founded on the rock." (Matthew 7:25) We must teach that righteousness through dependency on Christ is the only way to weather the Spiritual storms that will surly come and maintain a right relationship with Christ.

6. And he said to them, "Go into all the world and proclaim the gospel…" (Mark 16:15) Sharing the Gospel should become as natural as eating, sleeping, or talking with others about sports, shopping, or our families.

7. ". . . Go therefore and make disciples of all nations. . ." (Matthew 28:19) We must learn to teach and practice Christ like multiplication.

Developing Steps to Follow

Step 1: Inviting others to grow in their understanding and personal relationship with God *must be intentional*. However, we must look closely at Jesus' example and realize He never forced or manipulated a single person into following Him. In fact, He was so blunt in describing the difficult requirements that most often he ran people off. Keep in mind Jesus was seen as a rock star after having performed miracles. We don't have that benefit. For this reason, we must reveal as much of our personal relationship with Christ to others as we are humanly possible. In other words, we cannot be hidden disciples and expect anyone to follow us.

At the same time, Jesus was never arrogant in His approach. When He turns to the crowd in Luke 14, He is not beating His own chest but pointing to what His true disciples had already done in order to be His disciples.

Humility is a clear evidence of the Holy Spirit being in control of our lives and, regardless of the pedestal we are placed on in the eyes of others, we must recognize that the God who created all chose us to bear fruit. We did not choose to bear fruit on our own. Only when the Holy Spirit chooses to use us in the life of another and draws that person to become a disciple through us will true fruit be produced.

In no way, however, does this mean we have no obligation to be obedient to Christ's command to "go" and make disciples. The very intent of Jesus in using the verb "go" is that we realize this is not a command to open the doors of the church or our house and wait for someone to beg us to teach them. We must be intentional about getting out into the communities and asking others to join us in becoming disciples and growing our relationship with Christ.

Jesus in no way was random about this nor should we take the shot-gun approach to disciple making. It may be that in the church is the best meeting place, but we should never limit it to time or place. A classroom setting may be the easiest way and the most traditionally acceptable way, but it is not Jesus' way. When we set our hearts to do the work of making disciples in the same way Jesus did (John 14:12), we need to pay close attention to His example and His every day, every place approach should be our pattern.

Even before we can make a good plan to go and make disciples, we ourselves must make a firm commitment not to just make an attempt at it, but rather make a commitment to keep on going and seeking to make disciples until God trusts us enough to draw someone into our life to be discipled.

We must have already made a commitment and a plan to go all the way with that person until they are prepared to make disciples themselves.

Personal Evaluation:

    a. My personal approach to inviting another Christian to be a disciple is to:

Step 2: The investment a disciple maker must make requires both sacrifice and daily commitment. Jesus said it this way, **"If anyone would come after me, let him deny himself and take up his cross daily and follow me." (Luke 9:23)**

The question each disciple must answer is "What is my cross?" For most of us, it is denying our comfort, our privacy, and our self-centered lives. With all the comforts available to us today, our comfort zones are hundreds of miles wide and virtually inescapable. So maybe God does not want us completely out of that comfort zone. Maybe He wants to use that as part of the disciple-making process.

Think about it: If Jesus is in us, then wherever we are, He is also. If we make it all about denying what we have and where we live; we have also denied Christ the opportunity to choose to use us in the lives of those captive to comfortable places and things. Is it possible Jesus is Lord of all? Is it impossible for Him to use us in our comfort zones to draw other believers into a disciple's relationship? Could it be that the real cross a disciple bears is to wake up every morning and deny himself the right to choose where and when and in whom God will use him? Could it be that, instead of us adapting to discomfort in order to understand the Lordship of Christ, we can simply deny who we are and take up the cross of servant to our Lord right where we are? We do not have to go on a mission trip or travel to distant lands and adapt to different cultures in order to submit to the Lord and let Him choose to use us where He desires.

Yes, God will send some to distant lands and completely out of their comfort zones. However, it will not be because that is the only place He is Lord, but rather because He can trust that disciple with the lives of those in a different culture. So maybe our cross is to stop waiting for God to send us at all and simply be submissive to His control wherever we are.

There is one factor that we need to recognize and be willing to accept: The risk factor. Jesus reminds us to count the cost in Luke 14. Though He does not specifically spell out the risk factors, we simply have to look at the lives of His disciples to see the great risk and understand the cost of giving our whole life to Christ. When we place our faith in Christ, it becomes natural to trust Him. But when we are investing our lives in others, we must maintain our faith solely in Christ alone. The real key to investing your whole life into another is to give yourself to that person without putting your faith in that person. This is the biggest risk you will take because disappointment can kill the heart of a disciple maker. The truth is that men will disappoint you, so plan to keep your faith in and focused on Christ.

Personal Evaluation:
    a. These are the things I will do in order to invest my life in the life of a potential disciple:

Step 3: Identifying spiritual birth is necessary for the disciple making process to grow and mature. When Jesus describes the spiritual birth to Nicodemus in John 3, He makes it clear that though we cannot expect to explain spiritual birth, we can identify it by the effects of it. In other words, we should not feel the need to argue that we have experienced spiritual birth but rather simply point to the effects that spiritual birth has had on our lives.

We cannot have experienced spiritual birth without there being some identifiable effect or evidence of the Spirit's work in our lives. As we teach others to see those spiritual evidences in themselves and others, we must be careful not to point them to physical or material changes that have come through human desire. If a person simply stops wearing clothes that identify them with an obvious sinful lifestyle, it in no way is evidence of spiritual birth. However, if the wardrobe change is accompanied by an attitude change that forces the person away from friends and places that perpetuate the sinful lifestyle, it could be pointed to as evidence.

Evidence of real spiritual birth is always eternal and most often will not be accepted by the world at large. For instance, hunger for knowledge of Scripture is an obvious evidence of spiritual birth. But only someone who had experienced a lack of hunger or desire for God's Word and then, as a result of spiritual birth, they unexplainably gain a deep desire to understand and retain it will fully comprehend what has taken place in the life of another.

Scripture itself is the best judge of spiritual birth because it identifies some of what spiritual birth produces in every life. Look at Galatian 5 and you will find a list of evidence that may be present in a person who has not been born of the Spirit. Then, starting in verse 22 you will see a list of evidence, called fruit of the Spirit, which will be present in the person who has been born of the Spirit.

The ability to see and identifying fruit of the Spirit becomes a continual reminder of spiritual birth. When we as disciples are able to identify not just life changes but also fruits or evidence that the Spirit is at work in our lives, we have no need to worry or wonder about it again. We should accept the truth of spiritual birth and give the Spirit the freedom to produce His fruit in us, no longer letting the world of spiritually dead folks cast doubt in our heads.

Personal Evaluation:
a. The best way for me to teach others to understand and identify their own spiritual birth is to:

Step 4: Leading others into a right relationship with our Lord Jesus Christ is what disciples should be about. This means we must first have and maintain a right relationship ourselves. Jesus lived His relationship with the Father in front of His disciples. He continually reminded them of the fact that the relationship between God the Son and God the Father was as close as it can be. Listen closely to what Jesus says about the relationship in John 14:10-11:

> *"Do you not believe that I am in the Father and the Father is in me? The words that I say to you I do not speak on my own authority, but the Father who dwells in me does his works. Believe me that I am in the Father and the Father is in me, or else believe on account of the works themselves."*

We must be willing to put down the religious flags and language and both follow and teach this relationship as the most important aspect of every disciple's life. When we are so tuned in to the person of Jesus that our thoughts and even our choice of words are as if He Himself were talking, then we can say, **"The Lord and I are one."** This is the relationship that we as disciple makers must work toward and lead others to work toward.

Within John 14 and 15, Jesus gives us all the instructions, tools, and ability to have a right relationship with God. Our job is to learn and practice the instructions until we realize the relationship of being one with Him. Then we will be prepared to experience the promised Holy Spirit working in and through us.

Jesus credits God's Holy Spirit as being the source of our authority to do great works. Disciples don't just talk about how the Holy Spirit works in their lives but, just like Jesus, the Holy Spirit at work in us becomes evident to those around us. As we teach the relationship, this central promise must be at the core of everything we teach; Apart from the Holy Spirit we can do nothing.

Memorize Jesus' promise, **"And I will ask the Father, and he will give you another Helper, to be with you forever, even the Spirit of truth, whom the world cannot receive, because it neither sees him nor knows him. You know him for he dwells with you and will be in you." (John 14:16 & 17)** Write it on your hearts. Talk about it day and night. Teach it to all other believers. Seek for it to be the reality of your relationship with God.

"In that day you will know that I am in the Father, and you are in me, and I am in you."

(John 14:20)

Personal Evaluation:

    a. The way I personally will teach others how to have a right relationship with God is to:

Step 5: Taking an in-depth look at Matthew 5-7, we learn the truth that **righteousness** is only obtained through complete dependence on God! We must recognize that the Sermon on the Mount is much more crucial to our everyday walk as disciples than any other single passage of scripture. If we are to experience the Kingdom of God, if we are to live in it each day, we must do much more than lump it into a sermon package and call it good. We must look at the way Jesus structured the text and aligned the principles. We must make it a personal declaration that we submit to. We must see it as Jesus saw it, as the constitution of the Kingdom that will dictate a righteous life here and now and throughout eternity.

As disciple makers, we should realize that teaching righteousness is fundamental. Jesus is not simply laying out a set of good suggestions for us to consider and choose to adhere to or not. Jesus is reading from God's handbook. If this were not so, Jesus would have left it up to us and our human conscience to do what is right. He does not leave us condemned to our own lack of wisdom. Here in Matthew, He spells it out in black and white with no room for a gray margin in which to experiment or test righteousness.

The tendencies of most disciple makers are to lead others toward a dependency on a local church and or the paid staff. This is not always a bad move and in fact, if the staff is equipped and prepared to disciple someone to a greater extent, it very well may be the best way. However, we must at the very least draw those God has trusted to us into a basic understanding of Matthew 5:3-12.

In particular, a correct and full understanding of what and who Jesus means by, "Blessed are the poor in spirit…" is imperative. (Matthew 5:3) Keep in mind, Jesus was not entrusting this to the theologians of the day, but fishermen, carpenters, and tax collectors. Examine who Jesus is teaching in this passage and you will understand that God selects the one who understands spiritual poverty to teach spiritual poverty. It may be that God has chosen you for this step in the disciple making process and He will use other disciple makers to teach other steps.

This makes it imperative that we learn and practice the key to all righteousness: **full dependence on God.** The rest of this constitution will merely serve to frustrate and cause confusion for the ones who attempt to keep it apart from spiritual dependence.

Personal Evaluation:

a. How I plan to use Matthew 5 through 7 to teach righteousness to others is to?

Step 6: Disciple makers teach others to **build an evangelical lifestyle** as Jesus demonstrated in His daily life with His disciples. Jesus had the Kingdom of God as the primary topic of every conversation. At times, He was straightforward and blunt, for example, with the rich young ruler or the man who wanted to get his house in order before committing. At other times, He was softer and asked questions, for example, of the Samaritan woman at the well. These stories right out of Jesus' ministry serve as teaching lessons for every disciple of Christ.

Maybe the greatest example that has become lost in our busy world is discussing evangelism with our brothers and sisters in Christ. Just look how excited the disciples were upon the return from their first mission trip in Luke 10:17. Sharing our evangelism experiences with other believers needs to become an everyday practice. The newly married man wants to show off his bride to every member of the family as well as the world of strangers. The new mother is so proud of her baby she can't help but share it with all her relatives, along with those in the supermarket and in the park. The grandparent boasts photos and talks constantly about their grandchildren like they can do no wrong. The disciple should be just as excited to share the one whom they have brought to salvation in Christ and the first place he should share him or her is among the Christian family.

Even our attempts that do not yield fruit should be discussed so we together can evaluate and encourage each other. If there is a spirit of love among the family of believers then no one should be ashamed of the Gospel or talking about his or her experiences in sharing it. There is only one of two reasons this is not a common practice during church fellowships and Sunday morning gatherings. One is that very few ever share their faith and the Gospel or second, we are afraid of how other Christians will react to our evangelical habits. Both speak to our lack of love for God and His Gospel.

A Christ-like evangelical lifestyle is much more than going out witnessing on occasion. It is more than going on mission once a year. It is more than sharing our experiences with other Christians at church. A true Christ-like evangelical lifestyle will draw us to those who need Christ and draw those in need of a savior to the Christ that lives in us.

There are four very key elements of an evangelical lifestyle that we should teach and demonstrate in our own lives:

1. Practice daily;
2. Be non-judgmental (reach out to all people);
3. Be unashamed (not concerned about what other think of us);
4. Be saturated with sincere Love.

Personal Evaluation:
   a. In teaching others to build a lifestyle of evangelism I plan to:

Step 7: **Multiplication** sounds complicated, but it very well may be the easiest and most critical part of making disciples. Most disciple makers perceive multiplication as counting heads or those who have said a sinner's prayer. In fact, many church leaders track this like a sports tournament pitting Christians in a competition against each other. This is not at all what Jesus taught in regard to multiplication and will eventually lead to fewer disciples practicing any type of multiplication at all.

Before we share the Gospel and before we ask anyone to pray a sinner's prayer, our hearts and minds need to focus on God using us to change lives rather than count heads. It is imperative that we ourselves have and teach others to have a clear understanding that an attitude of multiplication, as it relates to making disciples, means reproducing our disciples' lives, not merely convincing someone to believe as we believe and saying, "I hope to see you in heaven one day." This starts with us being sure and comfortable as Disciples of Christ and worthy to be followed.

If our minds and hearts are right with Christ and we are prepared to be followed and teach others to live a Christ-like life worthy of following the Holy Spirit, Christ must do all the hard work of drawing to us those who can and will be multiplying disciples. This takes away the burden of pressuring ourselves into counting heads and places the multiplication process squarely on God's shoulders.

In practical terms, let's say two disciple makers, Joe and Tom, set out to multiply. Joe is one of those disciple makers that has a deep desire to multiply, understands it is not about numbers, and feels he can best do that by setting a modest goal of making at least one disciple a year. Tom is a good disciple maker just like Joe in every way except one. Tom does not set a goal to make one disciple a year but rather he sets a goal to teach one disciple to be a disciple maker who teaches a disciple to be a disciple maker and so on every year.

At the end of 20 years, Joe has been very successful at making his one disciple a year and has successfully produced 20 sound disciples. Tom has also been very successful and as a result of teaching his disciples to make and teach others to make disciples, he has over one million disciples directly related to his understanding of multiplication. One disciple makes a disciple each year and therein multiplies via addition. The other multiplies disciples by teaching every disciple to make and teach their disciple to make disciples and thereby adds and multiplies through those he has added.

Tom is not in competition with Joe and, in fact, has himself made no more disciples than Joe. So, the question then is how many disciples would be made if we as disciple makers encouraged each other to understand Godly multiplication?

Personal Evaluation:

    a. My plan to teach and assist in the multiplication of disciples is:

Are You Truly a Disciple?

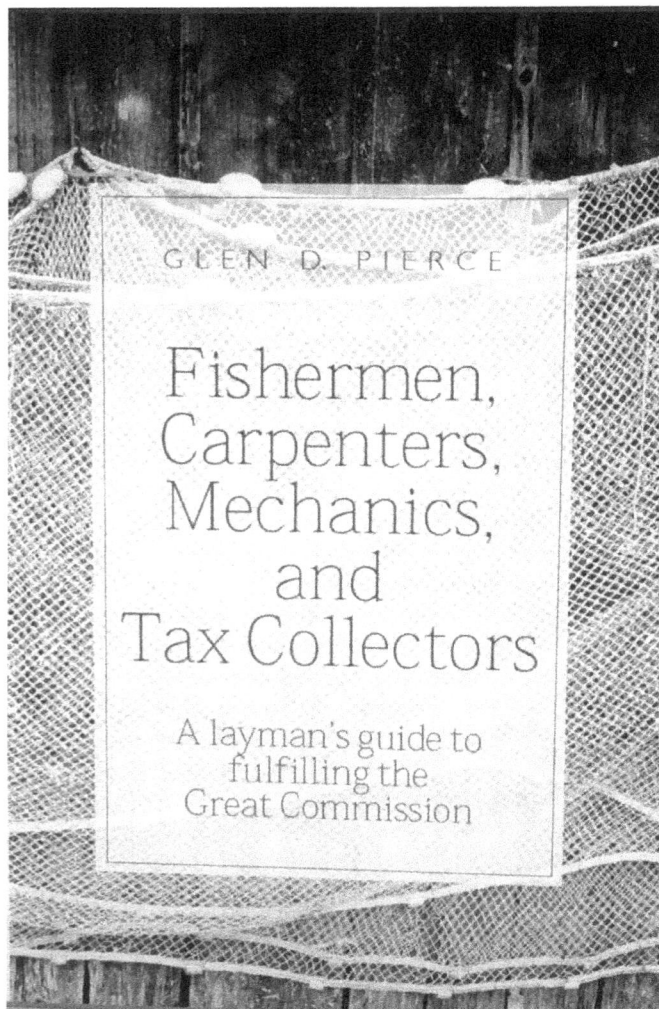

Glen D. Pierce seeks to teach others the importance of having a contagious personal relationship with Jesus. His book Fisherman, Carpenters, Mechanics, and Tax Collectors gives guidance and direction in the pursuit of not just becoming a Disciple of Christ but also in becoming a Disciple Maker who encourages and trains others to share Gods love and the Gospel around the world.

"The Kingdome is built in the streets by those who are willing to leave the Palace"

Matthew 28:19-20

www.ingramcontent.com/pod-product-compliance
Lightning Source LLC
Chambersburg PA
CBHW081513040426
42447CB00013B/3212